The Dominion of God
vs. The Dominance of Man

J. M. Muratore

Benjamite Publishing
Coeur D'Alene, Idaho

ISBN 979-8-218-63733-0 (paperback)

Edited by Audrey Eaves
Internal Design by Kadesh Ink Author Services

Printed in the U.S.A.

Benjamite Publishing
benjamitepublishing@yahoo.com

To God first,

And to everyone that prompted me to write this.

CONTENTS

CHAPTER ONE

Our God Is a God of Order

The greatest book ever written, the Bible starts with God explaining that "in the Beginning," He created. From the start, we are offered a complex understanding of God's dominion over space, matter, and time. It is order. Creational order. It's the foundation on which we build upon in all arenas of existence.

A look at the state of world affairs shows us that the world is being less covert in its wickedness than we remember it once being. Has sin come anew, or become greater? Is it not still the same sin as it was from the beginning? Why do things seem to be getting increasingly more wicked? God hasn't changed. Sin hasn't changed. God's Word is the same yesterday, today, and forever. So why is there so much chaos? Why is there so much disorder? What is happening in and with the church today?

What have relationships become? The world seems to have a definition for words like marriage, fatherhood, femininity, and woman. Why has the holy and righteous institution of marriage become something so common, mundane and trivial? Why is divorce so commonplace? Isn't marriage supposed to be a moral fixture—a holy, stable, and loving venture? Why have things become so laden with perversion? Polygamy, adultery, and polyamory—do these depict order and reflect godliness? At the time of my writing, only a few short months ago, the Pope, who is supposed to be a holy figure, was pushing for alternative lifestyle affirmations that take "Pride" in actions that the Bible calls a sin. Not long ago, the Baptist church was caught in a scandal regarding sexual abuse, its lies, and coverups.

There was a story even more recent about a disastrous flood displacing many and causing great hardship. As this was taking place, a certain well-known mega church pastor refused to unlock the doors to the tax-exempt facility. The place of sanctuary and worship refused to aid and accommodate the vulnerable with inescapable needs.

Then there is the increase of entertainment based "sermons", presented by preachers who zipline into the service to music by a secular artist renowned for displays of sexploitation at her concerts. To then stand before hundreds, even thousands of impressionable souls, telling you that the Bible is but a vehicle to deliver your desires and wants to you. We have many pastors who not only are entrenched in pornography but are the advocates of it privately for married couples. The holy union of marriage is ending in divorce at a rate of 40-50%. Does this sound like God's order? Does that sound like walking in righteous dominion?

With these distractions in the church, the wolves breed and multiply in too many pulpits, while scattered sheep are searching for truth after having found the church lacking. Heresies of old have arisen. Doctrines regarding polygamy and extra-biblical books have resurfaced. It is growing difficult in the minds of many believers to understand that what they have been passed down from generation to generation are often teachings *about* the Bible, rather than understanding that they are reading and hearing the very sacred Word of God. This has resulted in wide-ranging paradoxical doctrines that force the will of mankind into a position against the order of God. It is at its core a rebellion. A rebellion that is against its own purpose is itself a cancer. It is disorder and dysfunction.

Our people are perishing for both lack of knowledge and a lack of vision (Hosea 4:6; Proverbs 20:18). We have strayed from the order of God. We must return the focus away from ourselves and back to God. Not the god we built in our image using patchwork verses that buttress our comforts and sins. We must focus on repairing the breach (Isaiah 58:12) in the church, and to stand against the tide of wickedness enveloping us in this age. Focus and find renewed strength. Focus on the only true God of the Bible and who He says that He is...

... the God of order.

CHAPTER TWO

Fallen Dominion

Our God is a God of order. When we look at the first chapter of Genesis, what do we see? We see that "in the Beginning God created." The highest order, the pinnacle of power and authority. God created the heavens and the earth and then He created man. When we think about the creation of man back in the garden, God decided to make Man in His image. *He* made Man and gave him dominion over the earth. In the second chapter of Genesis, God outlines that He made the garden and gave Man purpose to tend to it. He made animals and brought them to the man that Adam might name them.

Was this dominion to control and oppress the creatures that God had just made in a form of harsh slave-ship? I don't think so. He created man and had him give all the animals names and man was to cultivate the earth. Cultivate, prosper, care for, and exercise dominion.

> Genesis 2:5 Now no shrub of the field was yet in the earth, and no plant of the field had yet sprouted, for the Lord God had not sent rain upon the earth, and there was no man to cultivate the ground.

The Lord God planted a garden toward the east, in Eden; and there He placed the man whom He had formed. Man's purpose before the fall was to exercise his dominion as a cultivator.

> Genesis 2:8-9;15 The Lord God planted a garden toward the east, in Eden; and there He placed the man whom He had formed. 9 Out of the ground the Lord God caused to grow every tree that is pleasing to the sight and good for food; the tree of life also in the midst of the garden, and the tree of the knowledge of good and evil. 15 Then the Lord God took the man and <u>put him into the garden of Eden to cultivate it and keep it</u>.

He wasn't oppressing the land by tending his dominion. He was operating in his Divinely assigned role. Genesis 2 was God giving Man dominion right beneath His own. Order, in His image. Take a moment on the weight of this matter and these deliberate actions of God. He's a God of order. God did not make woman first and give her this role of dominion over the earth. God did not make woman at the same moment as man to share in this dominion. Instead, Man was alone in his dominion and God said it wasn't good that he be in solitude/alone.

> Genesis 2:19-20 Out of the ground the Lord God formed every beast of the field and every bird of the sky, and brought them to the man to see what he would call them; and whatever the man called a living creature, that was its name. 20 The man gave names to all the cattle, and to the birds of the sky, and to every beast of the field, but for Adam there was not found a helper suitable for him.

Still within the dominion of Adam as a reflection of the Creator, he ruled and gave names to that which was in his dominion. God put a sleep over Adam and instead of creating independently from the dirt again as He had done with Adam, instead of giving the woman the same dominion and creation as Adam, God created her from Adam's rib.

> Genesis 2:21-23 So the Lord God caused a deep sleep to fall upon the man, and he slept; then He took one of his ribs and closed up the flesh at that place. 22 The Lord God fashioned into a woman the rib which He had taken from the man, and brought her to the man. 23 The man said, "This is now bone of my bones, And flesh of my flesh; She shall be called Woman, Because she was taken out of Man."

Who gives woman her name? Adam. Who gives Adam his name? God. The reflection of God is present in this creation. She is created by God and by Adam. Adam not only titles her woman but also gives her the name Eve, doing so by the role given to him by God in dominion. When God gave the command to not eat of the tree, He didn't give it to the woman.

> Genesis 2:15-17 Then the Lord God took the man and put him into the garden of Eden to cultivate it and keep it. 16 The Lord God commanded the man, saying, "From any tree of the garden you may eat freely; 17 but from the tree of the knowledge of good and evil you shall not eat, for in the day that you eat from it you will surely die."

God gave it to the man as the man was to be like the Bridegroom and lead his wife in the commands of God, just as Christ is the Bridegroom that leads us. Who was the first person to add to the command of God? The woman:

> Genesis 3:2-3 The woman said to the serpent, "From the fruit of the trees of the garden we may eat; 3 but from the fruit of the tree which is in the middle of the garden, God has said, 'You shall not eat from it or touch it, or you will die.'"

The woman was deceived by this addition to what God had stated. Yet, the Scripture points out that sin entered through Adam (Romans 5:12).

> Genesis 3:6-7 For God knows that in the day you eat from it your eyes will be opened, and you will be like God, knowing good and evil. "When the woman saw that the tree was good for food, and that it was a delight to the eyes, and that the tree was desirable to make one wise, she took from its fruit and ate; and she gave also to her husband with her, and he ate. 7 Then the eyes of both of them were opened, and they knew that they were naked; and they sewed fig leaves together and made themselves loin coverings.

The lie was that it would:
- open your eyes
- make you like God
- know good and evil

The temptation was that it was:
- "good for food"
- "delight to the eyes"
- "make one wise

One of the definitions of the Hebrew word know/*yada* is to declare. Mankind has been declaring "good" and "evil" instead of what God defines as good and evil, and this includes the roles given to us by God. Consider that Genesis 3 is about the Bride of Christ. God established His dominion and authority, as Christ has dominion and authority, but then we as the Bride through our temptation of self-determination and self-exaltation say, "no...". *We*, not God, are the ones who get to choose what is good and what is not. We say we are like God when we walk in rebellion to His authority. Then we establish OUR righteousness instead of His along this walk and falsely claim in newfound arrogance that it is also His.

We have opened our eyes to sin and have made ourselves like God in our declaration. It is for this reason there is such indignation by the Savior to the Pharisees who set aside the commands of God for the sake of their own traditions. As they go so far as to say that they declare what is and isn't food based on the ritual hand washing traditions of the elders. They delight in self-made wisdom rather than the wisdom of God, but we'll dive more deeply into that later.

For now, we are looking still at the dominion in Genesis and the headship of man.

Genesis 3:8-9 They heard the sound of the Lord God walking in the garden in the cool of the day, and the man and his wife hid themselves from the presence of the Lord God among the trees of the garden. 9 Then the Lord God called to the man, and said to him, "Where are you?"

As God is walking in the garden, does He call out "Egalitarian couple of equality, where would both of you be located?" No, He calls out to the man, as it was his duty and role to walk in the dominion of that which he was given. He called to the one who was entrusted with the command of God to lead his Bride. It is unmistakable that God called to him/Adam/the man.

Genesis 3:10-13 Adam said, "I heard the sound of You in the garden, and I was afraid because I was naked; so I hid myself." 11 And God said, "Who told you that you were naked? Have you eaten from the tree of which I commanded you not to eat?" 12 The man said, "The woman whom You gave to be with me, she gave me from the tree, and I ate." 13 Then the Lord God said to the woman, "What is this you have done?" And the woman said, "The serpent deceived me, and I ate."

Adam, instead of accepting the responsibility for his choice to disobey God, *blames his wife*, even though Adam was not the one deceived by the Serpent. Adam heard the command directly from the mouth of God, so there was no excuse. Adam had ceased to reflect the nature of God's guardianship by ignoring the word of God and in doing so, he surrendered his dominion.

Genesis 3:16 God to the woman He said, "I will greatly multiply Your pain in childbirth, In pain you will bring forth children; Yet your desire will be for your husband, And he will rule over you."

The judgement of God to the woman is that she will have pain in childbirth (which she still does) and Her desire will be for her husband (competing dominion) but He shall rule over her (dominion). Now there are some who would argue for different interpretations of what it means for the woman to have desire for her husband and him ruling over her. I've heard some that try to say that it's about sexual desire or any theory except for what is presented here. We know the correct meaning is that the desire is to be in dominion over her husband. The proof of this is found as it's used in the next chapter with Cain and his sin offering. Compare:

Genesis 3:16 To the woman He said, "I will greatly multiply Your pain in childbirth, In pain you will bring forth children; Yet your desire (**H8669** *tᵊšûqâ*) will be for your husband, And he will rule (**H4910** *māšal*) over you."

Genesis 4:7 If you do well, will not your countenance be lifted up? And if you do not do well, sin is crouching at the door; and its desire (**H8669** *tᵊšûqâ*) is for you, but you must master (**H4910** *māšal*) it."

But what does God say to the man?

11

Genesis 3:17-19 Then to Adam He said, "Because you have listened to the voice of your wife, and have eaten from the tree about which I commanded you, saying, 'You shall not eat from it'; Cursed is the ground because of you; In toil you will eat of it All the days of your life. 18 "Both thorns and thistles it shall grow for you; And you will eat the plants of the field; 19 By the sweat of your face You will eat bread, Till you return to the ground, Because from it you were taken; For you are dust, And to dust you shall return."

God states clearly that because Adam took the egalitarian position and handed over his dominion role to follow his wife's doctrine given to her by the serpent, that now his role is going to be exponentially harder. The ground is cursed because of Adam. The arena of his dominion has been infected. Everywhere he turns, his dominion will affront, challenge, and resist him. Did God change Adam's purpose or dominion in His rebuke? No. The charge is still the same for him even in exile. Genesis 3:23 ...therefore the Lord God sent him out from the garden of Eden, to cultivate the ground from which he was taken...

Now, in the context of Adam, the dominion of which he was supposed to lead, guard and care, he must now cultivate: the ground, which is polluted by sin because of Adam, and his wife, who was given to him to help reflect the image of God. Let's look at a few more passages.

Romans 5:12 Therefore, just as through one man sin entered into the world, and death through sin, and so death spread to all men, because all sinned

Eve did not doom humanity, Adam did. Adam is who is at fault because
Adam chose. It was his choice to heed counsel outside of what God had
commanded. He was not deceived.

Now look at 1 Timothy 2:

> Timothy 2:12-14 But <u>I do not allow a woman to teach or
> exercise authority over a man</u>, but to remain quiet. 13 <u>For it
> was Adam who was first created, and then Eve.</u> 14 And <u>it was
> not Adam who was deceived, but the woman being deceived</u>,
> fell into transgression.

It is stated that man is the covering over the woman just as the example
of the Father being over Christ, Likewise, as the King is over the Bride,
so is the husband over the wife. The royal kingdom set up of a king and
queen has the king ruling with the queen at his side—yet he is still the
one in dominion.

> 1 Corinthians 11:7-9 For a man ought not to have his head
> covered, <u>since he is the image and glory of God;</u> but <u>the
> woman is the glory of man.</u> 8 <u>For man does not originate from
> woman</u>, but <u>woman from man</u>; 9 for indeed <u>man was not
> created for the woman's sake, but woman for the man's sake.</u>

God did not create man to destroy the world, but to give him careful
dominion and stewardship that full prosperity may be maintained. The
reason that women are scripturally not permitted to be in authority over
men or to be pastors is that it is a direct reference to this truth. God
spoke to the man, man spoke to the woman. God led the man, man led

(or was supposed to) the woman. Now look at the example in Scripture even closer in this context of Ephesians 5:

> Ephesians 5:22-30 <u>Wives, be subject to your own husbands, as to the Lord.</u> 23 <u>For the husband is the head of the wife, as Christ also is the head of the church,</u> He Himself being the Savior of the body. 24 <u>But as the church</u> is <u>subject to Christ,</u> so also the <u>wives ought to be to their husbands in everything.</u>
>
> <u>25 Husbands, love your wives, just as Christ</u> also loved the church and gave Himself up for her, 26 so that <u>He might sanctify her,</u> <u>having cleansed her</u> by the washing of water with the word, 27 that He might present to Himself the
>
> church <u>in all her glory,</u> having no spot or wrinkle or any such thing; but that <u>she would be holy and blameless.</u> 28 <u>So husbands ought also to love their own wives</u> as their own bodies. He who loves his own wife loves himself; 29 for no one ever hated his own flesh, but <u>nourishes and cherishes it,</u> just as Christ also does the church, 30 because we are members of His body.

Just as Adam was given dominion to care for and steward the earth, he was given his wife to care for, watch over, to wash, and cleanse her—that is dominion language, not in an oppressive, pejorative way, but in a way of *love* and deep tender care *as he is to love his own flesh.*

Wives are still called like Eve, to submit to their husbands in everything and *resist* that desire to seize dominion over him. When a wife refuses to allow her husband's leadership per Divinely appointed call, she actively resists God and the reflection of the order that He put in place. It becomes a picture of Eve with the forbidden fruit all over again.

Genesis 1 establishes God's authority and dominion as Genesis 2 establishes Adam's with Genesis 3 being the bride and the fall. God commands Adam, Adam is head over Eve. A, then B, then C. The serpent inverses this order and everyone moves out of their place. The serpent gives Eve the doctrine, Eve eats, Eve gives to Adam, and he eats. "C", then "B", then "A". The authority dynamic shifts backwards from what God established. Adam was given dominion over all the earth, but, when he chose to eat the fruit, he surrendered that dominion to Satan. That's why Satan is said to be the prince of this world. In light of this... we see a direct parallel to the temptation of Christ. Satan tries to give Christ doctrine, Christ refuses the doctrine of the serpent, and Christ places God's dominion back in right order.

When women reject the order that God has set to reflect Him and His order and defiantly take to the pulpits declaring themselves to be pastors over men and congregations, they have absolutely and unequivocally eaten a doctrine from the adversary of which they have been deceived as being good for food, a delight to the eyes, and having made them wise.

CHAPTER THREE

Ezer Kenegdo

We've walked through the groundwork (pardon the pun) of what dominion means in regard to man. If man is given dominion over the earth as a cultivator to prosper and preside over it, then two questions arise: 1. What if man doesn't walk in the dominion that God has set; and 2. what about the woman?

The opposite of God-ordered dominion is dominance. I'll get into painstaking detail on that and how that is defined in the Scriptures soon, but let us first discuss the woman and what "*ezer kenegdo*" means. This is a term that I have seen floating around social media and championed by those who would wish to empower women in the ways and calling of men. Take a look around and compare our culture with what the word of God says we are to be and you'll see stark contrasts.

- We are seeing men trying to be women and women trying to be men.
- We're seeing attempts to rebrand and redefine marriage.
- We're seeing people attempting to say that men can get pregnant and have periods.
- We're seeing people attempt to redefine what love is rather than how God and His word define it.

We're to look at the Word of God and conform to it, not to our society around us. Our society has infiltrated the church and church structures and is trying to use the mask of sounding holy while pushing these cultural redefinitions. Why is it so important to talk about headship and authority? Because God structured it. Because we are called to be men and women of God! We are called to reflect *His* glory, which includes gender roles, the family structure, and how He ordered things to be done.

Many doctrines and ideas have been tossed around in my hearing and I usually just file them away in my mind under the heading of "something about this topic doesn't sound right: look into it later." The *"ezer kenegdo"* and the subject of biblical headship/authority was one of them. Though there is much to be said about men and how they need to die to themselves to lead like Christ Jesus, this chapter will address women specifically.

God: Keep the Sabbath.
Women: Ok.
God: Don't eat unclean.
Women: Ok.
God: Submit to your husband in everything.
Women: Woah, hold on there, Bud...what if...

What about this:

Women: Men should lead.
Women: To be in submission to a man's authority is slavery.

This dichotomy is a lose-lose for men that grinds away at the functionality God designed in their role as men. To understand the origins of headship and the functionality of men and women, we have to look at the first enactment thereof. Egalitarianism posits that the *ezer kenegdo/neged* is that Man and Woman are co-equal in the matters of Biblical authority. Is that what the text bears out?

Man was created and God saw this and said it is not good for man to be alone, so He made Eve.

> Genesis 2:18 Then the LORD God said, "It is not good for the man to be alone; I will make him a helper suitable for him."

The words used are *ezer*, and *neged*, but when used in a sentence, the grammar structure of the Hebrew renders it as *kenegdo*:

וַיֹּאמֶר יְהֹוָה אֱלֹהִים לֹא־טוֹב הֱיוֹת הָאָדָם לְבַדּוֹ 2:18
אֶעֱשֶׂה־לּוֹ עֵזֶר כְּנֶגְדּוֹ:

	Septuagint	Forward	Reverse	Fwd Inline	Rev Inline

English (NASB) [?]	Strong's	Inflected, Root & Transliterated	Parsing
a helper PHRASE	H5828	עֵזֶר / עֵזֶר / ēzer	HNcmsa
suitable for him PHRASE	H5048	כְּנֶגְדּוֹ / נֶגֶד / neḡed	HR/R/Sp3ms

What it means is a helper opposite of him.

19

adverb

II. in front of, straight forward, before, in sight of
III. in front of oneself, straightforward
IV. before your face, in your view or purpose

with preposition

V. what is in front of, corresponding to
VI. in front of, before
VII. in the sight or presence of
VIII. parallel to
IX. over, for
X. in front, opposite
XI. at a distance

preposition

XII. from the front of, away from
XIII. from before the eyes of, opposite to, at a distance from
XIV. from before, in front of
XV. as far as the front of

There are a few people who insist that the interpretation of the phrase "opposite to him" means equal in strength to oppose him. They use this because the term *ezer* is used in other places to denote military assistance, such as when God has rendered assistance in the times of Israel's wars. One big issue with this interpretation is that if we were to read into it that the woman is to be the "Xena" to his "Hercules", we are injecting a narrative into the understanding when this phrase merely means "helper" sitting across from him.

Stating that because the word *ezer*, "help" is used in places in reference to God "helping" Israel, then Adam receiving this "help" in the garden when woman is created to "help" man would make her a warrior, rather than a "help" in response to his being one person in a kingdom of pairs. This places woman in the position of God as the helper to Israel. If a child needs help putting their shoes on and a sibling helps (*ezer*) them, does this make the sibling fit for war and an equal authority in his parent's house? It does not. Eve wasn't there to wage war, she was put there to help. What war was there in the pre-fall garden? In fact, when we look at God's commands in Deuteronomy, it seems clear that woman is not supposed to be that warrior:

> Deuteronomy 22:5 "A woman shall not wear man's clothing, nor shall a man put on a woman's clothing; for whoever does these things is an abomination to the Lord your God.

This isn't just a point against cross dressing—one of the definitions for this verse is a warrior's garb- weaponry, and armor.

(5) *arms, weapons* (Rüstzeug), Gen. 27:3; more fully, מִלְחָמָה [כְּלֵי] Jud. 18:11, 16. כְּלֵי־מָוֶת deadly weapons, Psalm 7:14. נֹשֵׂא כֵלִים an armour-bearer, 1 Sa. 14:1, 6, 7, seq.; 31:4, 5, 6. בֵּית כֵּלִים an armoury (Zeughaus). Isa. 39:2.

The implication of the idea that woman is to be this co-warrior, masculine-style fighter is in direct conflict with other commands of God. To speculate that to be opposite of the man means to be equal in authority dismisses that the "curse/rebuke" God gives over the woman at the fall is: 1. Pain in conception; 2. pain in childbirth; and 3. the desire for her husband (directly leading to) and that instead He will RULE over her. The text states that the man will have dominion over the woman.

KJV Translation Count — Total: 81x

The KJV translates Strong's H4910 in the following manner: rule (38x), ruler (19x), reign (8x), dominion (7x), governor (4x), ruled over (2x), power (2x), indeed (1x).

Outline of Biblical Usage [?]

    I. to rule, have dominion, reign

      A. (Qal) to rule, have dominion

      B. (Hiphil)

        i to cause to rule

        ii to exercise dominion

Strong's Definitions [?]   (Strong's Definitions Legend

מָשַׁל **mâshal**, maw-shal'; a primitive root; to rule:—(have, make to have) dominion, governor, ✗ indeed, reign, (bear, cause to, have) rule(-ing, -r), have power.

That is synonymous with having authority over her. This is headship. As we continue, I'll show that this headship is still prescriptive in the New Testament and we'll highlight the difference between dominion and how it differs from dominance.

Whenever the subject of headship is brought up, many—and I'd go so far to say most women in our society and culture—picture a man dominating and controlling, an apocalyptic warlord type who rules by force and makes women his slaves. A loss of autonomy is usually what I hear most, that a wife becomes just an object or instrument for male gratification via fleshly goods and services.

THIS IS NOT THE BIBLICAL EXAMPLE OF THE WAY A MAN IS TO BE.

I'll probably say that a few times in this part of the book because a lot of conversations I have on this subject, no matter how many times I stress the point, the words are dismantled in someone's mind and reassembled in a way that sounds like "men should control women".

> Ephesians 5:22-24 Wives, be subject to your own husbands, as to the Lord. 23 <u>For the husband is the head of the wife</u>, as <u>Christ also is the head of the church</u>, He Himself being the Savior of the body. 24 But as <u>the church is subject to Christ</u>, so also <u>the wives ought to be to their husbands in everything.</u>

The husband is the head of the wife the way Christ is the head of the church. Does the church regard itself as an equal authority to Christ? Not unless you ascribe to certain Catholic views. As the church is subject to Christ (the church is acknowledging the Messiah's headship and authority), so also wives ought to be (submitted) to their husbands in everything. Most women who buck this are following the leadership of men that did not love them as Christ loves the church, men who refused to submit to Christ and to love their wives the way that Christ loves the church. Where these men lead an example of rebellion against the command of God to love their wives in *His* example, so too, do many women follow suit in not submitting to their husbands. The argument that sometimes comes up is "If he led like Christ, I would have no issue submitting to him". This is neither a good or accurate argument because Christ currently leads like Christ and we all still struggle with submitting to Him in everything. If God is an equal part in the marriage between two people, then the call for the woman to worship God in the way that God has prescribed is not incumbent upon the husband to be doing everything the way that Christ does, although he *absolutely should* do everything the way Christ commands.

<u>This is not about giving power or authoritarian control to men.</u> <u>This is not about enabling abuse by men—</u> <u>as those are NOT the example of Christ to His church.</u>

A husband has loving compassion for his bride, As Christ does the church.
A husband seeks input from his bride, As Christ does the church.
A husband gives sacrificially for his bride, As Christ does the church.
A husband gives good gifts and provides the righteous desires of his wife, as Christ does the church.
A husband guards against evil that seeks to destroy his family, As Christ does the church.
A husband leads his wife in the Word, As Christ does the church.
He's not a micromanager. As the example of Adam in the Garden with Eve, Eve ate the apple, but Romans says that sin entered through one man, Adam. When Adam sinned, God, who I believe knew that Eve ate the apple first, called out to Adam to account for his actions.

This is why Paul cites this in 1 Timothy:

> 1 Timothy 2:10-14 but rather by means of good works, as is proper for women making a claim to godliness. 11 A woman must quietly receive instruction with entire submissiveness. 12 But I do not allow a woman to teach or exercise authority over a man, but to remain quiet. 13 <u>For it was Adam who was first created</u>, and then Eve. 14 <u>And it was not Adam who was deceived</u>, but the <u>woman being deceived, fell into transgression.</u>

Paul isn't just tossing out an opinion. He's not being sexist. He's citing the authority role that is given to the man of headship. Men are to take input from their wives and attend to their needs, but when it goes wrong, that responsibility is on the shoulders of the man to have been doing what should have been done.

> 1 Peter 3:1-2 In the same way, you wives<u>, be submissive to your own husbands so that even if any of them are disobedient to the word</u>, they <u>may be won without a word by the behavior of their wives</u>, 2 as they observe your chaste and respectful behavior.

Of note is that these verses written to the wives of pagan husbands emphasize submission the most. Peter says that obedience is the way in which to win the unrighteous husband, not resistance.

<u>THIS IS NOT AN ENDORSEMENT FOR SUBJECTING TO ABUSE</u> .

This demonstrates that the Biblical patriarchy of male headship and authority in leading the wife is established, and that even the new converts should exemplify this in order to show God to their husbands. This is stated in Titus 2.

> Titus 2:4-5 so that they may encourage the young women to love their husbands, to love their children, 5 to be sensible, pure, workers at home, kind, being subject to their own husbands<u>, so that the word of God will not be dishonored.</u>

The word of God is dishonored when authority/headship/rule is wrestled from the man and the man is subdued under the woman as exactly what the "curse" in Genesis states. If Submission meant only giving way when you agree, that isn't submission that is agreement. That's bargaining. That word for "dishonored" is Greek: *blasphemo*. It means blasphemy. This reads that wives not being subject to their own husbands blaspheme the word of God. That is not an easy thing for our culture that champions feminism or egalitarianism.

TO BE CLEAR, SUBMITTING TO A HUSBAND IS NOT SLAVERY

Ephesians 5:28 In the same way, husbands should love their wives as **their own bodies**. He who loves his wife loves himself

This is not the attitude of someone who deprives another for amusement, but rather he gives to his wife in the way that he would give to himself. The husband makes judgments, like the example of Christ and the church. In making a judgment, he considers what is best for his wife and the family. He takes her counsel and input. He inquires of God about matters. He then makes a judgment. The judgment is not passing authority to his wife and submitting to her headship, it is a judgment in her favor championing the wisdom and good counsel that she has provided. If the wife offers good counsel and wisdom and the husband's judgment is to not listen to it, *then the reproach is on the husband.*

The Greek word for submit is *hypotassō* and it means:

Outline of Biblical Usage [?]

   I. to arrange under, to subordinate
   II. to subject, put in subjection
   III. to subject one's self, obey
   IV. to submit to one's control
   V. to yield to one's admonition or advice
   VI. to obey, be subject

In this example, *hypotassō* is:
To arrange under- the husband's authority.
To put in subjection- to the husband's authority.
To obey- one's husband's ruling.
To submit to one's control- the one being the husband.
To yield to one's admonition or advice- the one being the husband.
To obey/subject- to your husband.

Advocates of egalitarian "authority" innately in practice make null and void all other commands in Scripture of submission by over emphasizing that we are all to submit to each other. The verse cited for these grounds is in Ephesians:

> Ephesians 5:21 and subject yourselves to one another in the fear of Christ

It is easy to understand how one derives that we're to submit to one another and that the only headship/authority is Christ. Yet, if we take this at face value with no surrounding context, then the next two verses have no meaning:

> Ephesians 5-22-23 Wives, <u>subject yourselves to your own husbands,</u> <u>as to the Lord.</u> 23 <u>For the husband is the head</u> of the wife, as <u>Christ also is the head</u> of the church, He Himself being the Savior of the body.

Rather in the fuller context we see the practice of *communal* submission, as verse 15 points out:

> Ephesians 5:15 So then, be careful how you walk, not as unwise people but as wise.

It appears to go from communal households collectively submitting to each other as a community, to the specific commands to husbands and wives about headship and submission in marriage. If we were to interpret verse 21 as blanket headship, this then gives the entire neighborhood authority to govern the marriage between God, Man and Woman. I do <u>NOT</u> think that the community does or should have the *intimate* form of authority in the marriage between husband and wife.

Of the common arguments against the word headship meaning what the Greek defines it as saying, is to convey that headship means something else entirely. I've heard it expressed:

> *"Head doesn't mean authority, it actually means the source, like the head of a river. it's the source of its beginning."*

The problem with this is that the Greek does mean authority. The same Greek that is used in Ephesians 5 and 1 Peter 3 to say that wives should

submit to the authority of their husbands is also used in the Septuagint
for the following verses:

> Psalms 8:6 You have him <u>rule over</u> **H4910 / G5293** the works
> of Your hands; You have put everything under his feet

Rule over- Hypotassō

> Psalm 144:2 My faithfulness and my fortress, My stronghold
> and my savior, My shield and He in whom I take refuge, Who
> <u>subdues</u> **G5293** my people under me. -

H40 in theHebrew *Māšal,* is *Hypotasso* in the Greek as **G5293**

Again, *hypotassō* shows that rule is not "source", it is
authority/ruling/headship over. For a moment, let's indulge the analogy
of the river. If *hypotassō* was to mean source, it would be in the reference
of the authority flowing from the source of the husband to the wife.
Even if we were to not take *Hypotassō* to mean authority, headship, and
rulership the way that it does, we still have other Greek words that give
us this meaning, such as *kephalē,* as seen used in the Septuagint.

> Psalm 18:43 You have delivered me from the contentions of
> the people; You have placed me as <u>head</u> **G2776** of the nations;
> A people whom I have not known serve me.

David is not the source of the nations. He's placed in *kephalē*—authority
and leadership of the nations.

Isaiah 9:14-16 So the Lord cuts off head and tail from Israel, Both palm branch and bulrush in a single day. 15 The head **G2776** is the elder and honorable man, And the prophet who teaches falsehood is the tail. 16 For those who guide this people are leading them astray; And those who are guided by them are brought to confusion.

The head *kephalē* equates to the elder/honorable man leader, contrasted with the tail/fool, one who teaches falsehood.

Judges 11:8-9 The elders of Gilead said to Jephthah, "For this reason we have now returned to you, that you may go with us and fight with the sons of Ammon and become head **G2776** over all the inhabitants of Gilead." 9 So Jephthah said to the elders of Gilead, "If you take me back to fight against the sons of Ammon and the Lord gives them up to me, will I become your head **G2776**?

It wouldn't make sense to be asking "Can I become your origin/source" of all the inhabitants of Gilead or the Elders. It only makes sense in the context of becoming the authority/ruler/headship.

Judges 11:11 Then Jephthah went with the elders of Gilead, and the people made him head **G2776** and chief over them; and Jephthah spoke all his words before the Lord at Mizpah.

They made him the authority-head-chief-*kephalē*.

2 Samuel 22:44 "You have also delivered me from the contentions of my people; You have kept me as head G2776 of the nations; A people whom I have not known serve me.

A people that he has not known now serve him as head/authority/*kephalē*. The word is also used in 1 Corinthians:

1 Corinthians 11:3 But I want you to understand that Christ is the head G2776 of every man, and the man is the head G2776 of a woman, and God is the head G2776 of Christ.

Look at this same example without even using the Greek:

1 Kings 8:1 Then Solomon assembled the elders of Israel and all the heads of the tribes, the leaders of the fathers' households of the sons of Israel, to King Solomon in Jerusalem, to bring up the ark of the covenant of the Lord from the city of David, which is Zion.

Solomon isn't assembling all the sources of the tribes. The sources of all the tribes would just be Jacob. He's not piecing Jacob back together. He's assembling the authority, the leadership the *kephalē*

Outline of Biblical Usage [?]

    I. the head, both of men and often of animals. Since the loss of the head destroys life, this word is used in the phrases relating to capital and extreme punishment.

    II. metaph. anything supreme, chief, prominent

        A. of persons, master lord: of a husband in relation to his wife

        B. of Christ: the Lord of the husband and of the Church

        C. of things: the corner stone

We can see from def. 2.A. the Greek word for head is "Husband's authority in relation to his Wife", in the same manner of def. 2.B. that "Christ is the Lord of the husband and of the church". If we take the two words *ezer naged/kenegdo* to mean warrior of the same authority as her husband, then these examples lose meaning and these words lose meaning. Sarah the matriarch and wife of Abraham uses the same definition of 2. A. when she refers to Abraham as lord/master. This is cited in 1 Peter:

> 1 Peter 3:5-6 For in this way in former times the holy women also, who hoped in God, used to adorn themselves, <u>being submissive to their own husbands</u>; 6 <u>just as Sarah obeyed Abraham, calling him lord</u>, and you have become her children if you do what is right <u>without being frightened by any fear.</u>

It's been suggested that doing this very thing would be like essentially abandoning autonomy and just becoming like an inanimate doll or a plaything to a man. While I understand the fear in that assessment, is that the example we see from Sarah and Abraham's relationship? What we see is quite the opposite in the Hagar situation. Sarah wanted Hagar gone. Did Sarah remove Hagar, who was her maidservant? No. Sarah brought the matter up to her husband in submission. Abraham wasn't wanting to send Hagar away, as we can see in the text that shows he was really bothered by this.

> Genesis 21:10-13 Therefore she said to Abraham, "Drive out this maid and her son, for the son of this maid shall not be an heir with my son Isaac." 11 <u>The matter distressed Abraham greatly because of his son.</u> 12 <u>But God</u> said to Abraham, "Do

not be distressed because of the lad and your maid; whatever <u>Sarah tells you, listen to her,</u> for through Isaac your descendants shall be named. 13 And of the son of the maid I will make a nation also, because he is your descendant.

What did He do? *He submitted to God the way Sarah submitted to him.* God was the one who made the ultimate decision: "Do what your wife is asking of you". Sarah got her way. Sarah was not without voice. She was not a slave. Abraham loved his wife the way that Christ loves the church. Yeshua in the Garden of Gethsemane didn't *want* to go to the cross, but He prayed as an example of perfect submission to the Father "your will be done, not mine", and *then gave up his life for us.*

Again, in 1 Corinthians 11, we see this headship, the *kaphale*, translated by many as "authority", stated outright:

> 1 Corinthians 11:3 But I want you to understand that <u>Christ is the head</u> [kephalē] of every man, and the man is the head [kephalē] of a woman, and God is the head [kephalē] of Christ.

Christ is the authority over every man, and man over [his] woman. This is in direct contradiction of the egalitarian interpretation that the woman's authority is equal to her husband. The egalitarian mindset of *ezer naged/kenegdo*. It points back to the context that woman is the help of man. Just as Esau despised his birthright and traded it for stew, women in our culture have traded this gift of being cared and provided for, loved, cherished, and valued with the ability to love and sow into a husband. They have traded it for genuine slavery to the corporate machine and employers that they're forced to submit to in a way that they fear from a husband.

So many women in the church think that submitting to their husbands is a form of slavery, but they do not think this same thing about submitting to Christ, and Christ says to submit to your husbands! That is obedience to Christ.

IT'S NOT ABOUT DOMINANCE
AND CONTROL TO THE MAN...

... it's about trusting God and having faith in God that the man you chose to marry is going to also be obedient to the God that you serve and trust. There are examples of male headship and authority all over the Scriptures as direct commandments from God.

> Numbers 30:3-5 Also if a woman makes a vow to the Lord, and binds herself by an obligation in her father's house in her youth, 4 and her father hears her vow and her obligation by which she has bound herself, and her father says nothing to her, then all her vows shall stand and every obligation by which she has bound herself shall stand. 5 But if her father should forbid her on the day he hears of it, none of her vows or her obligations by which she has bound herself shall stand; and the Lord will forgive her because her father had forbidden her.

By the male headship/authority of the father, the woman breaking a vow is not under penalty because the father has nullified it. Think about this for a moment. Think about how we as people in rebellion to God the Father have made a covenant with Death, but our Father has chosen to nullify that vow. This same authority set up is for husbands to wives:

> Numbers 30:6-8 However, if she should marry while under her vows or the rash statement of her lips by which she has bound herself, 7 <u>and her husband hears of it</u> and says nothing to her on the day he hears it, then her vows shall stand and her obligations by which she has bound herself shall stand. 8 <u>But if on the day her husband hears of it, he forbids her, then he shall annul her vow</u> which she is under and the rash statement of her lips by which she has bound herself; and the Lord will forgive her.

How many women commit to something they wish they hadn't and wish they could get out of it? Try biblical headship/authority. Think about this in the context of us as the Bride of Messiah and how we each have made the covenant with Death through our rebellion against God. His grace nullified the rashness of our lips. This passage on the nullification of vows show that the egalitarian co-head authority position isn't Divinely structured. This is not the *ezer naged/kenegdo* Xena warrior mindset. She is someone across from him reminding him always to be more like the Messiah, to die to self, to love, to submit to God in his actions the way or greater than the way she is submitting to him. She serves him, and along with him, rather than warring against him like the "curse" states.

Even if we were for some wild reason to outright ignore both Greek words talking about the husband's headship, we still have it from Numbers 5 that says that the wife is under the authority of her husband.

The word husband is added to the text by translators, a practice that I don't normally endorse, but the context is clear that it is an appropriate translation.

> Numbers 5:19-20;29 The priest shall have her take an oath and shall say to the woman, "If no man has lain with you and if you have not gone astray into uncleanness, <u>being under the authority of your husband</u>, be immune to this water of bitterness that brings a curse; 20 if you, however, have gone astray, being <u>under the authority of your husband</u>, and if you have defiled yourself and a man other than your husband has had intercourse with you" This is the law of jealousy: when a wife<u>, being under the authority of her husband</u>, goes astray and defiles herself-

Even if we were for some reason to outright ignore both Greek words talking about the husband's headship, *and* ignore the passage in Numbers, we still have it from God as shown above and from Genesis itself.

> Gen 3:16 To the woman He said, "I will greatly multiply your pain in childbirth, In pain you shall deliver children; Yet your desire will be for your husband, <u>And he shall rule over you</u>."

TWOT Reference: 1259

KJV Translation Count — Total: 81x

The KJV translates Strong's H4910 in the following manner: rule (38x), ruler (19x), reign (8x), dominion (7x), governor (4x), ruled over (2x), power (2x), indeed (1x).

Outline of Biblical Usage [?]

- to rule, have dominion, reign
  - A. (Qal) to rule, have dominion
  - B. (Hiphil)
    - to cause to rule
    - to exercise dominion

God expressly states that the husband does in fact rule as one with authority. That same word is used when God warns Cain:

> Genesis 4:7 "If you do well, will your face not be cheerful? And <u>if you do not do well, sin is lurking at the door; and its desire is for you, but you must master</u> **(H4910)** it."

Do you see the parallel of "The Desire will be over your husband" and "Sin is lurking with Desire for you", and the parallel between "And he will rule over you" with "you must master it"? It is the same word of overcoming in regards to authority. When we state to Christian brothers and sisters that obedience to God's Law is love (Deuteronomy 11:1, John 14:15;21, John 15:10), they so often reply that "The Law is bondage". We who walk in God's Law know that obedience is freedom (James 1:25, James 2:12) and the lie of it being bondage becomes almost laughable. It's a delight to bask in the joy of our God (1 John 2:3-4, Psalm 119:92). The world tells us that same lie about marital submission, calling it bondage and slavery. And a note to men: if you are dominating your wife in an authoritarian power trip, *repent, because you are doing evil and it is a hindrance to your prayers to God.*

> 1 Timothy 5:8 But if anyone does not provide for his own, and especially for those of his household, he has denied the faith and is worse than an unbeliever.

> 1 Peter 3:7 You husbands in the same way, live with your wives in an understanding way, as with someone weaker, since she is a woman; and show her honor as a fellow heir of the grace of life, so that your prayers will not be hindered.

Which brings us to the opposite of dominion...dominance

CHAPTER FOUR

The Pre-Existence of God's Law

Building on the previous chapters showing what God's Dominion is, what Man's created purpose is, what is ordered authority as it pertains to the wife...we're now going to set a quick foundation in order to define what results when Men forsake that created purposes of reflecting God's glory in being cultivators and to obey the Divine command of being fruitful and multiplying.

There are various labels for the doctrines that people make when they look at Scriptures to try and reconcile certain passages with other passages based on their best understanding. Some people break the Word up into dispensations and periods where God was different to people at one point, and then He changed and in the New Testament He's a more laid-back God who is relaxed with everyone. A huge problem with this is that God says many, many times that He doesn't change.

> Exodus 3:14 God said to Moses, "I Am who I Am"; and He said, "Thus you shall say to the sons of Israel, 'I AM has sent me to you.'"

Malachi 3:6 "<u>For I, the Lord, do not change</u>; therefore you, O sons of Jacob, are not consumed.

Numbers 23:19 "<u>God is not a man, that He should lie, Nor a son of man, that He should repent</u>; Has He said, and will He not do it? Or has He spoken, and will He not make it good?

1 Samuel 15:29 Also the Glory of Israel <u>will not lie or change His mind</u>; for He is not a man that He should change His mind."

Psalm 102:27 "But <u>You are the same</u>, And Your years will not come to an end.

James 1:17 Every good thing given and every perfect gift is from above, coming down from the Father of lights, <u>with whom there is no variation or shifting shadow</u>.

In the Exodus 3 passage, God is stating that He is now as He will be—He causes Himself to exist and will remain as He is. What this means is that the God of Genesis who, rather than smite Adam and Eve for their rebellion against His decree and Him scooping up new dirt and starting over, chose to extend grace out of His own compassion by promising a Savior. The very moment that God gave humanity probation rather than death, Grace was on display and has been in the world from its foundations. What this also means is that when God gave His laws and standards of what is holy, and what is not holy, this was not in contradiction nor contention with the grace of God, but in conjunction with it. We see the harmony of grace and God's commandments/Law throughout the Scriptures, but, specifically for this portion, I need to highlight that there are certain things we can confirm were already established *before* Sinai and the giving of the Torah.

Psalm 81:3-5 <u>Blow the trumpet at the new moon</u>, At the full moon, on our feast day.4 For it is a statute for Israel, An ordinance of the God of Jacob. 5 <u>He established it for a testimony in Joseph When he went throughout the land of Egypt.</u> I heard a language that I did not know:

Genesis 7:1-5 Then the Lord said to Noah, "Enter the ark, you and all your household, for you alone I have seen to be righteous before Me in this time. 2 You shall take with you of <u>every clean animal</u> by sevens, a male and his female; and <u>of the animals that are not clean two</u>, a male and his female; 3 also of the birds of the sky, by sevens, male and female, to keep offspring alive on the face of all the earth. 4 For after seven more days, I will send rain on the earth forty days and forty nights; and I will blot out from the face of the land every living thing that I have made." 5 Noah did according to all that the Lord had commanded him.

Gen 6:21 As for you, take for yourself some of <u>all food which is edible</u>, and gather it to yourself; and it shall be for food for you and for them."

Gen 4:3-5 So it came about in the course of time that Cain <u>brought an offering to the Lord</u> of the fruit of the ground. 4 Abel,<u> on his part also brought of the firstlings of his flock and of their fat portions.</u> And the Lord had regard for Abel and for his offering; 5 but for Cain and for his offering He had no regard. So Cain became very angry and his countenance fell.

Exodus 16:4-5 Then the Lord said to Moses, "Behold, I will rain bread from heaven for you; and the people shall go out and gather a day's portion every day, that I may test them, whether or not they will walk in My instruction. 5 On the sixth day, when they prepare what they bring in, it will be twice as much as they gather daily."

Exodus 18:16 When they have a dispute, it comes to me, and I judge between a man and his neighbor and make known the statutes of God and His laws."

Leviticus 23:24 is when the written command is given for the New Moon celebration of which Joseph and Israel were keeping before Sinai. In Exodus 18, we have Moses making known God's Laws in his rulings and judgements. In Exodus 16, we have God seeing if Israel will obey His laws. In Genesis 7, we have the existence of clean and unclean animals long before their written list in Leviticus 11. Genesis 4 has Cain and Abel offering sacrifices and offerings far before the Temple, Tabernacle, or Levitical priesthood. This practice had to come from somewhere. I believe it came from our unchanging God who tells us what is Holy in His Kingdom and what is not.

When people think of God's Law, what is often spoken is that God gave His Law to the Jews. Have we considered that God is not a respecter of persons? Why would He only give His standard of what is Holy and unholy and make that only apply to one specific tribe of one specific set of people? Does that make sense in light of the fact that sin is violating the commands of God? Does the God of order who created mankind to reflect His image in His glory—Our God who so loved the world that He gave His only Son to redeem all who believe—have a different set of commands for one people than the other? If you've ever read the book of Leviticus or Numbers, or if you have ever read the details God goes into about how exactly to build the Tabernacle in Exodus, you know that God has no problem letting Man know exactly what is pleasing to Him and how he should obey. As God is a God of order, why would we think that from the moment we left the garden, it was all guess work as to what God would like and dislike?

Why would we think that our unchanging God would like obedience in the garden, only a specific people to be obedient outside of the garden, and then in the New Testament, everyone be obedient again but to a new and different playbook? That's not the picture that He portrays in the Biblical text.

God has repeatedly shown His dominion and rulership in what is good and pleasing to Him from the start, and it wasn't only for the Jews. Continuing on with examples of the pre-existence of God's Law, let's look at Job:

> Job 1:1-3 <u>There was a man in the land of Uz whose name was Job</u>; and that man was blameless, upright, fearing God and turning away from evil. 2 Seven sons and three daughters were born to him 3 His possessions also were 7,000 sheep, 3,000 camels, 500 yoke of oxen, 500 female donkeys, and very many servants; <u>and that man was the greatest of all the men of the east.</u>

Job was the greatest of all the men of the east right, according to the text. But what does that mean? Who are these east people? Where are they mentioned? Well, they existed around in Jacob's time:

> Genesis 29:1 Then Jacob went on his journey, and came to the land of the sons of the east.

The Midianites were from Abraham's other family in the remarriage after Sarah.

> Genesis 25:1–2 Now Abraham took another wife, whose name was Keturah. 2 She bore to him Zimran and Jokshan and Medan and Midian and Ishbak and Shuah.

So do the Scriptures show that Midianites are the sons of the east?

> Judges 6:33 Then all the Midianites and the Amalekites and the sons of the east assembled themselves; and they crossed over and camped in the valley of Jezreel.

> Judges 7:12 Now the Midianites and the Amalekites and all the sons of the east were lying in the valley as numerous as locusts; and their camels were without number, as numerous as the sand on the seashore

> Judges 8:5 He said to the men of Succoth, "Please give loaves of bread to the people who are following me, for they are weary, and I am pursuing Zebah and Zalmunna, the kings of Midian. Now Zebah and Zalmunna were in

Karkor, <u>and their armies with them</u>, about 15,000 men, <u>all who were left of the entire army of the sons of the east</u>; for the fallen were 120,000 swordsmen. 11 Gideon went up by the way of those who lived in tents on the east of Nobah and Jogbehah, and attacked the camp when the camp was unsuspecting. 12 When Zebah and Zalmunna fled, he pursued them and captured <u>the two kings of Midian, Zebah and Zalmunna</u>, and routed the whole army.

1 Kings 4:29-30 Now God gave Solomon wisdom and very great discernment and breadth of mind, like the sand that is on the seashore. 30 Solomon's wisdom surpassed <u>the wisdom of all the sons of the east</u> and all the wisdom of Egypt.

Isaiah 11:13-14 Then the jealousy of Ephraim will depart, And those who harass Judah will be cut off; Ephraim will not be jealous of Judah, And Judah will not harass Ephraim. 14 They will swoop down on the slopes of the Philistines on the west; <u>Together they will plunder the sons of the east</u>; They will possess Edom and Moab, And the sons of Ammon will be subject to them.

Ezekiel 25:9-10 therefore, behold, I am going to give you to the sons of the east for a possession, and they will set their encampments among you and make their dwellings among you; they will eat your fruit and drink your milk. 10 and I will give it for a possession along with the sons of Ammon <u>to the sons of the east</u>, so that the sons of Ammon will not be remembered among the nations.

If Job was from the sons of the east, and the sons of the east are Midianites, why would that be important for the point of establishing the pre-existence of the Law of God?

> Exodus 18:4-5 Now <u>Jethro, the priest of Midian, Moses' father-in-law</u>, heard of all that God had done for Moses and for Israel His people, how the Lord had brought Israel out of Egypt. 5 Then Jethro, Moses' father-in-law, came with his sons and his wife to Moses in the wilderness where he was camped, at the mount of God.

Jethro was a Midianite priest.

> Exodus 18:8-12 <u>Moses told his father-in-law all that the Lord had done to Pharaoh and to the Egyptians for Israel's sake, all the hardship that had befallen them on the journey, and how the Lord had delivered them.</u> 9 <u>Jethro rejoiced over all</u> the goodness which the Lord had done to Israel, in delivering them from the hand of the Egyptians. 10 <u>So Jethro said, "Blessed be the Lord</u> who delivered you from the hand of the Egyptians and from the hand of Pharaoh, and who delivered the people from under the hand of the Egyptians. 11 <u>Now I know that the Lord is greater than all the gods; indeed, it was proven when they dealt proudly against the people."</u> 12 Then <u>Jethro, Moses' father-in-law, took a burnt offering and sacrifices for God,</u> and Aaron came with all the elders of Israel to eat a meal with Moses' father-in-law before God.

Jethro learned about the Exodus, Passover, all of it... and he praised and offered sacrifices to YHVH, YeHoVaH, the Name of the God of Abraham, Issac, and Jacob.

> Exodus 18:13-16 It came about the next day that Moses sat to judge the people, and the people stood about Moses from the morning until the evening. 14 Now when Moses' father-in-law saw all that he was doing for the people, he said, "What is this thing that you are doing for the people? Why do you alone sit as judge and all the people stand about you from morning until evening?" 15 Moses said to his father-in-law, "Because the people come to me to inquire of God. 16 When they have a dispute, it comes to me, and I judge between a man and his neighbor and make known the statutes of God and His laws."

This is before Moses went up the mountain of Sinai, when Moses had the statutes and laws of God and He was making them known to the people.

> Exodus 18:17-23 Moses' father-in-law said to him, "The thing that you are doing is not good. 18 You will surely wear out, both yourself and these people who are with you, for the task is too heavy for you; you cannot do it alone. 19 Now listen to me: I will give you counsel, and God be with you. You be the people's representative before God, and you bring the disputes to God, 20 then teach them the statutes and the laws, and make known to them the way in which they are to walk and the work they are to do. 21 Furthermore, you shall select out of all the people able men who fear God, men of truth, those who

hate dishonest gain; and you shall place these over them as leaders of thousands, of hundreds, of fifties and of tens. 22 Let them judge the people at all times; and let it be that every major dispute they will bring to you, but every minor dispute they themselves will judge. So it will be easier for you, and they will bear the burden with you. 23 If you do this thing and God so commands you, then you will be able to endure, and all these people also will go to their place in peace."

Jethro the Midianite, who has just sacrificed and worshiped YHVH(God) for defeating the Egyptians, tells Moses to teach the statutes and the laws to men that they may walk the walk of obedience to God.

Exodus 18:24-27 So Moses listened to his father-in-law and did all that he had said. 25 Moses chose able men out of all Israel and made them heads over the people, leaders of thousands, of hundreds, of fifties and of tens. 26 They judged the people at all times; the difficult dispute they would bring to Moses, but every minor dispute they themselves would judge. 27 Then Moses bade his father-in-law farewell, and he went his way into his own land.

Jethro the Midianite heard directly from Moses' own mouth everything that God had done. He offered sacrifices to God and then instructed that the statutes and the ways of God be taught to others, and then Jethro returned to Midian, the place of the sons of the east.

While there are various thoughts on the matter, my personal belief at the time of writing this is that Job lived during Moses' lifetime. Many scholars disagree with each other as to when exactly Job was written, but that has no effectual change on anything for our sake in this understanding. It changes nothing because either way, the commands of God are in pre-existence and being practiced by a Gentile either before or at the time of Sinai. The same standard of God is applied. God's order is universal. Now we have established that the Law of God and the Commands of God existed prior to Exodus 19 and Moses ascending on Sinai.

> Malachi 2:10-12 "Do we not all have one father? Has not one God created us? Why do we deal treacherously each against his brother so as to profane the covenant of our fathers? 11 Judah has dealt treacherously, and an abomination has been committed in Israel and in Jerusalem; for Judah has profaned the sanctuary of the Lord which He loves and has married the daughter of a foreign god. 12 As for the man who does this, may the Lord cut off from the tents of Jacob everyone who awakes and answers, or who presents an offering to the Lord of hosts.

To recap, God established His authority, order, and His dominion over everything. God gave man dominion over the earth. God established His order and His standards of what is righteousness. We have discussed the model of headship and authority of the husband as it relates to being like Christ to his wife. We have discussed what it looks like for us as the Bride of Messiah, as for brides to their husbands, to submit to that authority. We have discussed the purpose for that order is to cultivate and be fruitful and multiply so that we may best reflect the glory and image of God in how we were created.

Having established all of this, I think we are now ready to discuss the opposite of dominion, the opposite of being cultivators that represent godliness. We're ready to discuss domination...the Nephilim.

CHAPTER FIVE

A Scripturally-Based Profile of the Nephilim and the Sons of God

I don't know if it is possible to discuss this subject without it getting a little weird. To discuss who and what the Nephilim are, we must inevitably discuss the sons of God and who they are. To discuss what the Nephlim are, it's going to get weird. Not the interdimensional hyper spiritualized type of weird. No, more the "Humans can be so gross" kind of weird. What I intend to do is to use Scripture to showcase who and what the Nephilim are, as Scripture is authoritative. We are commanded in the Scriptures to not add or take away from the Bible, so I do my very best to find answers from the established 66 canonized books. I firmly believe that the answers are in the Bible. Yet, people often look outside of the Bible to other writings for perspectives of which they filter the Scriptures through. This is not good practice. I do not recommend looking at other non-biblical texts to try to understand actual Biblical text. I'll get into more detail on the authenticity of God's word in a later chapter.

There are two main theories circulating about who the Nephilim were and who were the sons of God. Based on texts that are not the Bible, some have interpreted sons of God to mean fallen angels and the Nephilim as to be the sons of those fallen angels. This is basically the fallen angel theory and it's derived from the apocryphal book of Enoch. Those who disagree with that interpretation are usually labeled as holding the Sethite view, that the sons of God were just a righteous lineage of Seth who replaced the murdered Abel as a son of Adam. However, what I see and will show is that neither of these views are accurate. It's not about lineage at all, it's heart posture and obedience. The only lineage element is when the consequences of unrepentant sins of the fathers are being adapted as sins of the sons also, genetically. Are you ready to get weird? There's a lot to get through, so let's get started.

What does "Nephilim" mean?

נ.פ.יל nᵉphîyl, nef-eel'; or נ.פ.ל nᵉphil; from H5307; properly, a feller, i.e. a bully or tyrant:—giant.

esenius' Hebrew-Chaldee Lexicon [?]

נְפִיל only in pl. נְפִילִים m. *giants*, Gen. 6:4; Nu. 13:33. So all the ancient versions (Chald. נְפְלָא the giant in the sky, i. e. the constellation Orion, plur. the greater constellations). The etymology of this word is uncertain. Some have compared نَسِيل, نَسِيل, which Gigg. and Cast. render, great, large in body; but this is incorrect; for it means, excellent, noble, skilful. I prefer with the Hebrew interpreters and Aqu. (ἐπιπίπτοντες) falling on, attacking, so that נְפַל is of intransitive signification. Those who used to interpret the passage in Genesis of the fall of the angels, were accustomed to render נְפִלִים *fallers, rebels, apostates.*

The root word shows it's not about sky giants, but it's about those who fall away from obedience and faith, ceasing to be cultivators. Instead, they become destroyers—hunters.

Those who hold the fallen angels viewpoint might ask, "What about the Orion constellation, surely that means that they fell from space like fallen angels wouldn't it?" While I understand how one might come to that conclusion, no, I do not believe that is what it is referring to.

> Matthew 2:2 "Where is He who has been born King of the Jews? <u>For we saw His star in the east </u>and have come to worship Him."

It continues:

> Matthew 2:7-10 Then Herod secretly called the magi and determined <u>from them the exact time the star appeared.</u> 8 And he sent them to Bethlehem and said, "Go and search carefully for the Child; and when you have found Him, report to me, so that I too may come and worship Him." 9 After hearing the king, <u>they went their way; and the star, which they had seen in the east, went on before them until it came and stood over the place where the Child was.</u> 10 When they saw the star, they rejoiced exceedingly with great joy.

Why did they know that this star was proclaiming the birth of the Messiah?

Genesis 1:14 Then God said, "<u>Let there be lights in the expanse</u> <u>of the heavens</u> to separate the day from the night, and <u>let them</u> <u>be for signs and for seasons and for days and years</u>

This is not astrology, this is biblical astronomy in the order of God. What is the imagery of Orion's constellation? Orion is the constellation for the hunter. As the Hebrew-Chaldee Lexicon states, it is incorrect to ascribe the Nephilim to be large in body over the definition of being bully/tyrant/ hunters that strike down—fellers of men and armies. Make no mistake, there are giants in the Bible and I'll get to the "large in body" in a moment. First, we can see the definitions as cast down like excommunication or cut down like death, as in extinguishing a life, or in some respects to seemingly just lay down as in surrender like one would in abandoning the faith. Fallen from grace. Look at this word God uses and its various meanings when addressing Cain in Genesis 4:6:

(*d*) *to fall upon* as an enemy, *to attack*, Job 1:15; followed by בְ Jos. 11:7.—(*e*) *to alight* from a beast or chariot; followed by מֵעַל Gen. 24:64; 2 Ki.

HIPHIL —(1) causat. of Kal No. 1 *to cause to fall*, i. e.—(*a*) *to cast, to throw* (werfen) e. g. wood on the fire, Jer. 22:7; *to throw down, to prostrate* any one (niederwerfen), Deu. 25:2; *to throw down*, a wall, 2 Sa. 20:15.—(*b*) *to cause* any one *to fall by the* sword, Jer. 19:7; Dan. 11:12; *to fell* trees,

1. to fall, lie, be cast down, fail
   1. (Qal)
      1. to fall
      2. to fall (of violent death)
      3. to fall prostrate, prostrate oneself before
      4. to fall upon, attack, desert, fall away to , go away to, fall into the hand of
      5. to fall short, fail, fall out, turn out, result
      6. to settle, waste away, be offered, be inferior to
      7. to lie, lie prostrate
   2. (Hiphil)
      1. to cause to fall, fell, throw down, knock out, lay prostrate
      2. to overthrow
      3. to make the lot fall, assign by lot, apportion by lot
      4. to let drop, cause to fail (fig.)
      5. to cause to fall

What is man *supposed* to do and be? A cultivator shepherd who protects and prospers that which entrusted into his care. What is the opposite of that? A hunter, killer, bully, tyrant. We can see examples of these hunters who reject the ways of God and embrace actively walking contrary to them. Who is the first bully, tyrant, feller of men? Cain.

Genesis 4:8-12 Cain told Abel his brother. And it came about when they were in the field, that Cain rose up against Abel his brother and killed him. 9 Then the Lord said to Cain, "Where is Abel your brother?" And he said, "I do not know. Am I my brother's keeper?" 10 He said, "What have you done? The voice of your brother's blood is crying to Me from the ground. 11 Now you are cursed from the ground, which has opened its mouth to receive your brother's blood from your hand. 12 When you cultivate the ground, it will no longer yield its strength to you; you will be a vagrant and a wanderer on the earth." Then Cain went out from the presence of the Lord, and settled in the land of Nod, east of Eden.

As we established in the previous chapters, Cain was warned by God about what was good and pleasing according to His authority. Cain was told outright that sin sought to rule over him. Cain rejected the dominion that God ordered him to walk in and instead chose dominance over his brother. He rejected God and hated his brother because his brother's deeds were righteous and his were not.

> 1 John 3:11-12 For this is the message which you have heard from the beginning, that we should love one another; 12 not as Cain, who was of the evil one and slew his brother. And for what reason did he slay him? Because his deeds were evil, and his brother's were righteous.

Look at the way that Cain parallels Esau:

> Genesis 27:39-41 Then Isaac his father answered and said to him, "Behold, away from the fertility of the earth shall be your dwelling, And away from the dew of heaven from above. 40 "By your sword you shall live, And your brother you shall serve; But it shall come about when you become restless, That you will break his yoke from your neck." 41 So Esau bore a grudge against Jacob because of the blessing with which his father had blessed him; and Esau said to himself, "The days of mourning for my father are near; then I will kill my brother Jacob."

Cain was jealous of Abel because of the blessing of the Father and he sought to kill his brother—and did. He was cursed to wander. Comparatively, Esau the hunter was jealous of Jacob because of the blessing of the father and sought to kill his brother, bearing a grudge, and he was cast away from the fertility of the earth to wander.

It isn't a lineage that made men Nephilim, it is actions. It is a heart posture that abandons faith and walks in the ways contrary to God.

> 1 John 3 :12 not as Cain, who was of the evil one and slew his brother. And for what reason did he slay him? Because his deeds were evil, and his brother's were righteous

Whose son was Cain? Was he not Adam's son? The designation of being a son of the Evil one is based on *action*.

> Genesis 4:1 Now the man had relations with his wife Eve, and she conceived and gave birth to Cain, and she said, "I have gotten a manchild with the help of the Lord."

Cain was born to Adam and Eve but he was cut off from the family based on his actions and rejection of the ways of God. He *became* a killer, tyrant, bully, mighty one, feller of his brother...He became a Nephilim. The son of Cain followed in his father's footsteps in the rejection of the ways of God, as Lamech engages in polygamy and murder:

> Genesis 4:19-24 Lamech took to himself two wives: the name of the one was Adah, and the name of the other, Zillah. ... 23

Lamech said to his wives, "Adah and Zillah, Listen to my voice, You wives of Lamech, Give heed to my speech, <u>For I have killed a man for wounding me; And a boy for striking me</u>; 24 If <u>Cain is avenged sevenfold, Then Lamech seventy-sevenfold</u>."

If you have a group of people who have rejected the commands of God and are engaging in a flesh-based, polygamist family model, and having kids that are also rejecting the ways of God and engaging in ungodly relations, you're *not* getting a lot of genetic variance.

Genesis 4:26 To Seth, to him also a son was born; and he called his name Enosh. **Then men began to call upon the name of the Lord.**

"There are some who translate this verse, **to call themselves by the name of the Lord.** *This would indicate* **that people were defying God by attributing deity to themselves.** *If this is the case,* <u>*this verse may refer to the heathen idolatry that started at this time.*</u>*" - Don Stewart Blue Letter Bible*

What does this present to us? It shows us the rebellion against God. It can make the case that Lamech is also a bully, tyrant, and feller of men. It can show us the violent culture of those who reject God's ways. It can show us those who are embracing a fleshly lifestyle. God's pattern of marriage that was established at creation is one man and one wife.

Genesis 2:24 For this reason <u>a man</u> shall leave his father and his mother, and be joined to <u>his wife</u>; and they shall become <u>one flesh</u>.

58

It doesn't say that man shall be joined to "wives" and become one flesh; there is no plurality.

> Matthew 19:5 and said, 'For this reason <u>a man</u> shall leave his father and mother and be joined to his <u>wife</u>, and <u>the two</u> shall become <u>one flesh</u>'?

Again, a man, a wife, the two people, becoming one flesh. God never explicitly commands people to take multiple wives. We do have Him prohibiting it:

> Deuteronomy 17:17 **He shall not multiply wives for himself**, or else **his heart will turn away**; nor shall he greatly increase silver and gold for himself.

Taking multiple wives is contrary to the example of Christ returning for His bride. He doesn't return for His *brides*. He's coming for the one bride, the apple of his eye. What those who have rejected the ways of God have patterned is: one man and...whatever that man wants. Look at the son of Lamech, Tubal-cain:

> Genesis 4: As for Zillah, she also gave birth to Tubal-cain, <u>the forger of all implements of bronze and iron</u>; and the sister of Tubal-cain was Naamah.

Cain, who murdered his brother, has Lamech, who also is a murderer more so than his father, who has Tubal-cain, *who becomes an arms dealer*. Alright, maybe not an arms dealer, but he's definitely making swords and the point stands. Lamech rejected God's pattern of marriage and engaged in the polygamy in flesh-based domination.

> Leviticus 18:18 <u>You shall not marry a woman in addition to
> her sister</u> as a rival while she is alive, to uncover her nakedness.

Esau follows that same pattern of rejection of God's dominion and
instead seeks to establish a fleshly dominance.

> Genesis 28:8-9 So <u>Esau saw that **the daughters of Canaan
> displeased his father**</u> Isaac; 9 and Esau went to Ishmael, **and
> married, besides the wives that he had**, <u>Mahalath the
> daughter of Ishmael</u>, Abraham's son, the sister of Nebaioth.

Esau, just like great uncle Lamech. Esau despised his birthright. He
despised the ways of the Father. He was a hunter, much like...

> Genesis 10:8-10 Now Cush became the father of Nimrod; he
> became <u>a mighty one on the earth</u>. 9 He was <u>a mighty hunter</u>
> before the Lord; therefore it is said, "Like <u>Nimrod a mighty
> hunter</u> before the Lord." 10 <u>The beginning of his kingdom was
> Babel</u> and Erech and Accad and Calneh, in the land of Shinar.

> 1 Chronicles 1:10 Cush fathered Nimrod; <u>he began to be a
> mighty one</u> on the earth.

Nimrod was a hunter and he became a mighty one on the earth. Now
hold on a second. He became a mighty one? It was these killers and
tyrants that became the mighty ones of old mentioned in Genesis 6...

Genesis 6:4 <u>The Nephilim</u> were on the earth in those days, and also afterward, when the sons of God came into the daughters of men, and they bore children to them. <u>Those were the mighty men who were of old</u>, men of renown.

What does Nimrod mean?

   I. Nimrod = "rebellion" or "the valiant"

     A. the son of Cush, grandson of Ham, and great grandson of Noah; a mighty hunter, he established an empire in the area of Babylon and Assyria

It means "rebellion". The Nephilim were mighty men of old, and Nimrod *began* to be one of these mighty men. If this were the fallen angel theory, then that would mean that Nimrod, halfway through his life, would have to decide to be reborn as offspring of the fallen angels. It makes a lot more sense if you see it for what the text points to: Nimrod began to be a bully, tyrant, murderer. He became a man of rebellion as Nimrod was a "mighty one".

Genesis 6:4 states that the mighty ones were men of renown. Men. Men of violence. He was a hunter just like Esau who wanted to kill his brother. He was in rebellion like Cain who rejected the ways of God. He founded Babylon which was a testament to man instead of God. I maintain that the designation of the Nephilim is referring to a man of violence. The fact that we can see the lineage of Nimrod whose father was Cush, who became a Nephilim/ mighty one, tells us that the giants in Moses' day were humans, not fallen angel half human hybrids.

I know, there are giants in the Bible, I said I would get to that. There's time like the present, so let's look at Goliath, as he was one of these mighty ones.

> 1 Samuel 17:4-7 <u>Then a champion came out from the armies of the Philistines named Goliath</u>, from Gath, whose height was six cubits and a span. 5 He had a bronze helmet on his head, and he was clothed with scale-armor which weighed five thousand shekels of bronze. 6 He also had bronze greaves on his legs and a bronze javelin slung between his shoulders. 7 The shaft of his spear was like a weaver's beam, and the head of his spear weighed six hundred shekels of iron; his shield-carrier also walked before him.

The average height of man in the United States is 5ft 9in. The average weight of gear and armor for the United States Army infantry man is 120 lbs of gear. Goliath's gear was about 200 to 300 lbs for a man of 7 to 9ft in height. He was a destroyer, one that made a reputation as a champion of the Philistines, a killer, a feller of armies and men. Goliath was a descendant of Anak.

- Numbers 13 states that there were men of great size and there were the Nephilim
- Numbers 13 connects the Nephilim with the sons of Anak (the Anakim)
- Joshua 11 notes that the Anakim were driven into Gaza, Gath, and Ashdod.
- 1 Samuel 17 says Goliath was from Gath and that he was a giant.

Why are there giants? Why do they have six fingers and toes? The answer to this is so simple it's easy to overlook. Sin. The wages of sin and the curses that come from rebellion against God. Let's look at the curses that come from rejecting God's dominion and instead choosing to become a man of warlike dominance in hostile rebellion to God. Deuteronomy 27 lists some of the curses.

- Cursed is he <u>who dishonors his father or mother</u>.' And all the people shall say, 'Amen.'
- 'Cursed is he who <u>strikes his neighbor in secret</u>.' And all the people shall say, 'Amen.'
- 'Cursed is he who accepts a bribe <u>to strike down an innocent person</u>.' And all the people shall say, 'Amen.'
- <u>'Cursed is he who does not confirm the words of this law by doing them</u>.' And all the people shall say, 'Amen.'

It continues in the next chapter, Deuteronomy 28:

- "The Lord will send upon you curses, confusion, and rebuke,<u> in all you undertake to do, until you are destroyed and until you perish quickly, on account of the evil of your deeds, because you have forsaken Me</u>. 21 <u>The Lord will make the pestilence cling to you until He has consumed you from the land </u>where you are entering to possess it. 22 <u>The Lord will smite you with consumption and with fever and with inflammation</u> and with fiery heat and with the sword and with blight and with mildew, and they will pursue you until you perish
- "<u>If you are not careful to observe all the words of this law</u> which are written in this book, <u>to fear this honored and awesome</u>

name, the Lord your God, 59 then the Lord will bring
extraordinary plagues on you and your descendants, even severe
and lasting plagues, and miserable and chronic sicknesses.

Sin and rebellion against the ways of God. Rebellion and hostility
against faith in God and against loving God. Rejection of walking with
God in whom all His paths are peace results in disease and hereditary
afflictions, such as but not limited to: gigantisms, which is a tumor on
the pituitary gland, and polydactyly, which is extra fingers and toes.
Both of which still exist *to this day*.

Deuteronomy 28 gives us reasons for the genetic attributes of giants- but
it is the *choice of action and the rejection of God and God's ways that make
them Nephilim*. If you have God-given laws which state you're not to be
incestuously sleeping with your mother or sister and you're ignoring
these commands out of a spiteful hatred of the things of God, then your
offspring is not going to have a lot of genetic variances. If you are
walking in the curses that God laid out as a spiritual cause and effect,
you are going to be predisposed to hereditary diseases, just like God says
in Deuteronomy about the sins of the fathers being passed down.

Romans 1:24 24 Therefore God gave them over in the lusts of
their hearts to impurity, so that their bodies would be
dishonored among them.

Studies have shown this to be the case with issues such as alcoholism,
that the children of alcoholics have a greater disposition to alcoholism.
Look back at the context of Genesis 6:

Genesis 6:31 Now it came about, when men [human men] began to multiply on the face of the land, and daughters were born to them [secular daughters of these human men], 2 that the sons of God [believers] saw that the daughters of men[secular women] were beautiful; and they took wives for themselves, whomever they chose. 3 Then the Lord said, "My Spirit shall not strive with man [human men] forever, because he also is flesh [still human men]; nevertheless his days shall be one hundred and twenty years."

Men were being led away from the faith and obedience by enticing women. These once obedient sons of God (the church) were taking wives for themselves whomever they chose. One way to interpret that "whomever they chose" aspect might be that they were not following God's idea of marriage between one man and one wife, but were instead following Cain's son Lamech's example and choosing many wives, whomever they wanted. Regardless as to if it was many wives or being led astray by secular women that they were taking as wives, the point remains that they were leaving what was right and they were being led astray by these women...*just like with Balaam.*

Numbers 31:15 And Moses said to them, "Have you spared all the women? 16 Behold, these caused the sons of Israel, through the counsel of Balaam, to trespass against the Lord in the matter of Peor, so the plague was among the congregation of the Lord.

There was (and still is) a pattern of men ignoring what God has called them to do, in the way that they should walk, and abandoning the call to reflect the glory of God in which we were created to reflect. Instead, they went astray after the wayward women. Just like Adam in the garden. Let's continue in Genesis 6 with the exposition:

> Genesis 6: 4 The Nephilim [Hunter/ Bully / Tyrant/ Murderers] were on the earth in those days, and also afterward, when the sons of God came in to the daughters of men, and they bore children to them. **Those were the mighty men who were of old, men of renown**.

A visual timeline for things like this can be helpful, so I drafted this chart:

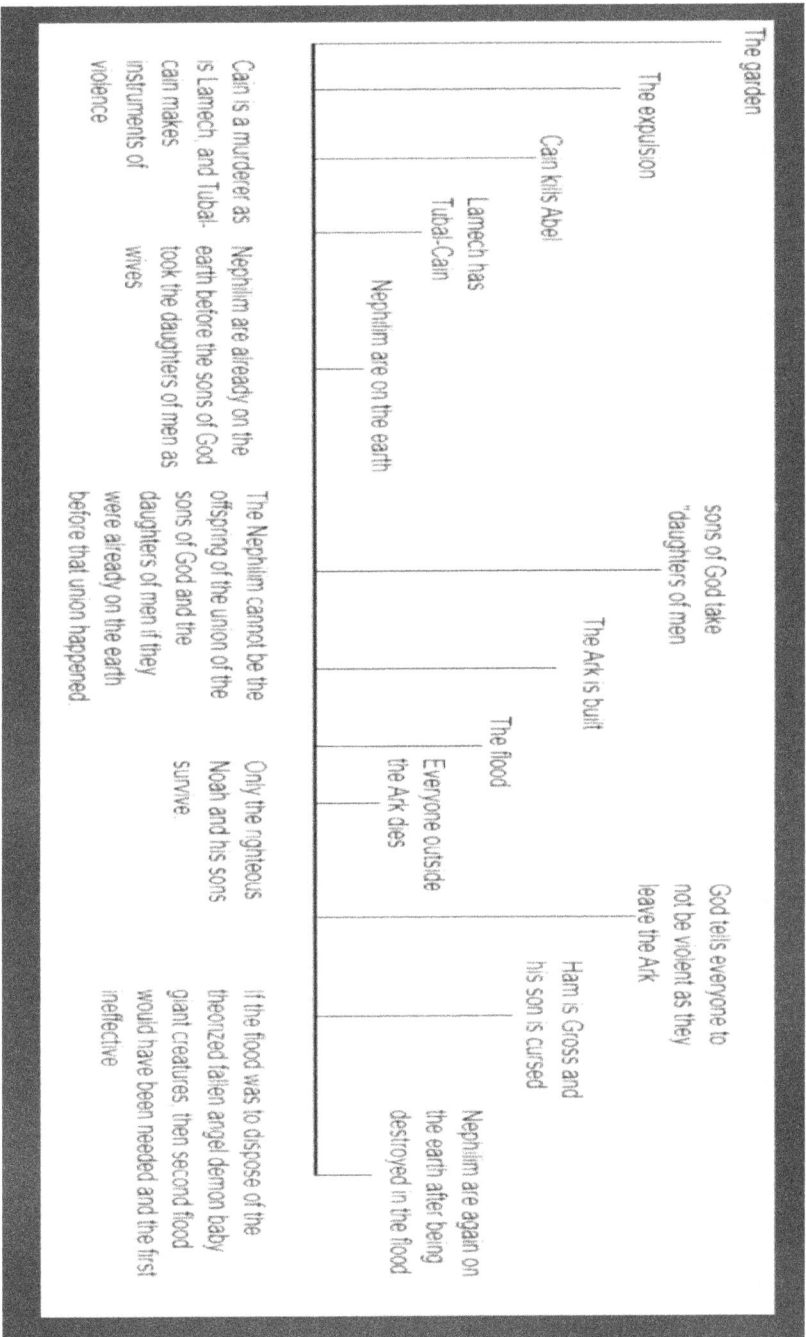

The garden

The expulsion

Cain kills Abel

Lamech has Tubal-Cain

Nephilim are on the earth

sons of God take "daughters of men"

The Ark is built

The flood

Everyone outside the Ark dies

God tells everyone to not be violent as they leave the Ark

Ham is Gross and his son is cursed

Cain is a murderer as is Lamech and Tubal-cain makes instruments of violence

Nephilim are already on the earth before the sons of God took the daughters of men as wives

The Nephilim cannot be the offspring of the union of the sons of God and the daughters of men if they were already on the earth before that union happened.

Only the righteous Noah and his sons survive.

If the flood was to dispose of the theorized fallen angel demon baby giant creatures, then second flood would have been needed and the first ineffective

Nephilim are again on the earth after being destroyed in the flood

Genesis 6:5-13 Then the Lord saw that the wickedness of man was great on the earth, and that every intent of the thoughts of his heart was only evil continually. 6 The Lord was sorry that He had made man on the earth, and He was grieved in His heart. 7 The Lord said, "I will blot out man whom I have created from the face of the land, from man to animals to creeping things and to birds of the sky; for I am sorry that I have made them." 8 But Noah found favor in the eyes of the Lord. 9 These are the records of the generations of Noah. Noah was a righteous man, blameless in his time; Noah walked with God. 10 Noah became the father of three sons: Shem, Ham, and Japheth.

11 Now the earth was corrupt in the sight of God, and the earth was filled with violence. 12 God looked on the earth, and behold, it was corrupt; for all flesh had corrupted their way upon the earth. 13 Then God said to Noah, "The end of all flesh has come before Me; for the earth is filled with violence because of them; and behold, I am about to destroy them with the earth

Adam was a shepherd, cultivator who bore the image of God. Abel was a shepherd and offered what was good and his deeds were righteous before God. Noah was a shepherd and found favor in the eyes of God, doing what is good, a preacher of righteousness. Jacob was a shepherd and cultivator who didn't choose multiple wives, he was tricked into it, and honored his vows to both women anyway. David was a shepherd and a cultivator before he was king.

Contrastly, Cain rejected the ways of God and became a killer—de-cultivator. Lamech was a polygamist and greater killer than Cain—de-cultivator. Esau rejected the ways of God and became a hunter—de-cultivator. Nimrod was a mighty one who made Babel in defiance of God and was a hunter—de-cultivator.

The fallen angel theory of the sons of God being angels at its core sounds absurd when you break it down to its elements.

Angels, who are constantly before God, rebelled against God. Although Scripture states God cast them into darkness in chains awaiting judgment, He allowed these fallen angels, who would now be classified as demons once they're exiled from heaven, allowed them to make a pit stop at earth and they somehow developed genitalia. Then, they entered into covenant sexual relationships with earthly women, as it says they took wives, not fornicated, with unmarried women, and sired offspring that resulted in half-angel, half-man giant demi god-like creatures. God opens and closes the womb. God knits creatures together in the womb, but we're supposed to believe that fallen angels who were kicked out of heaven and became demons were allowed to enter into covenant relationships with human wives and God opened their wombs and knit together a half-angel half-human hybrid that became a giant? That sounds like Greek mythology and Mt. Olympus. It doesn't sound like the sovereign God of the Bible. Furthermore, the fallen angels theory states that after the angels did this, that is why God wiped out everyone but Noah, in order to preserve a pure bloodline. Does that sound like the God of order? That He wiped out all the earth after making this mistake with the angels, *only* for the Nephilim to pop back up again *after* the flood? When we look at the entirety of the texts and we reason them together using the Scriptures instead of external, non-canon books that distort the doctrines of God, we can find clarity.

What we see is that Genesis 6 is not angel-demon babies being born and the union of spirits and women resulting in God killing all the men in the world for some reason, but it is about violence. What we see is that actions and choices are what makes one a son of God or an enemy of God. That's what makes one a Nephilim.

Even Josephus in the Antiquities of the Jews points to this in regard to Nimrod. He writes:

> "God also commanded them to send colonies abroad, <u>for the</u> <u>through peopling of the earth</u>; that <u>they might not raise seditions</u> <u>among themselves</u>, but might cultivate a great part of the earth, <u>and enjoy its fruits after a plentiful manner</u>. But they were so ill instructed, that they did not obey God. For which reason they fell into calamities, and were made sensible by experience of what sin they had been guilty of. For when they flourished with a numerous youth, God admonished them again to send out colonies. <u>But they imagining the prosperity they enjoyed was not</u> <u>derived from the favour of God, but supposing that their own</u> <u>power was the proper cause of the plentiful condition they were</u> <u>in, did not obey him.</u> Nay they <u>added to this their disobedience to</u> <u>the divine will,</u> the suspicion that they were therefore ordered to send out separate colonies, that, being divided asunder, they might the more easily be oppressed. 2. Now it was <u>Nimrod who</u> <u>excited them to such an affront and contempt of God.</u> He was the grand-son of Ham, the son of Noah: <u>a bold man, and of great</u>

strength of hand. He persuaded them not to ascribe it to God, as if it was through his means that they were happy; but to believe that it was their own courage which procured that happiness. He also gradually changed the government into tyranny; seeing no other way of turning men from the fear of God, but to bring them into a constant dependence on his own power. He also said, "He would be revenged on God, if he should have a mind to drown the world again: for that he would build a Tower too high for the waters to be able to reach; *and that he would avenge himself on God for destroying their fore-fathers.*"- Josephus Antiquities of the Jews 1.109–1.113 translated by William Whiston

[Disclaimer: Josephus is not Scripture and shouldn't be taken as Scripture, but he was a Jewish Historian documenting the thoughts and interpretations of his time]

Nimrod, this mighty one—this Nephilim—is creating violence against the ones who are obedient farmers and cultivators in the faith, for the purpose of getting them to reject God and become dependent upon his hand. Another way of saying this is that "the Nephilim were on the earth and made violence against God imposing tyranny and leading the sons of God astray".

1 John 3:10, By this the children of God and the children of the devil are obvious: anyone who does not practice righteousness is not of God, nor the one who does not love his brother.

Deuteronomy 14:1-2, You are the sons of the Lord your God; you shall not cut yourselves nor shave your forehead for the sake of the dead. 2 For you are a holy people to the Lord your God, and the Lord has chosen you to be a people for His own possession out of all the peoples who are on the face of the earth.

Romans 8:14 For all who are being led by the Spirit of God, these are sons of God.

Romans 8:19 For the anxious longing of the creation waits eagerly for the revealing of the sons of God.

Romans 9:25-27 As He says also in Hosea, "I will call those who were not My people, 'My people,' And her who was not beloved, 'beloved.'" 26 "And it shall be that in the place where it was said to them, 'you are not My people,' There they shall be called sons of the living God." 27 Isaiah cries out concerning Israel, "Though the number of the sons of Israel be like the sand of the sea, it is the remnant that will be saved."

Galatians 3:26, For you are all sons of God through faith in Christ Jesus.

Galatians 4:6, Because you are sons, God has sent forth the Spirit of His Son into our hearts, crying, "Abba! Father!"

Luke 6:35, But love your enemies, and do good, and lend, expecting nothing in return; and your reward will be great, and you will be sons of the Most High; for He Himself is kind to ungrateful and evil men.

1 Chronicles 17:13-16, <u>I will be his father and he shall be My son</u>; and <u>I will not take My lovingkindness away from him</u>, as I took it from him who was before you. 14 <u>But I will settle him in My house and in My kingdom forever</u>, and his throne shall be established forever.”’” 15 According to all these words and according to all this vision, so Nathan spoke to David. 16 Then David the king went in and sat before the Lord and said, “Who am I, <u>O Lord God</u>, and what is my house that You have brought me this far?”

Luke 20:34-36 Jesus said to them, “<u>The sons of this age</u> marry and are given in marriage, 35 but <u>those who are considered worthy to attain to that age and the resurrection from the dead</u>, neither marry nor are given in marriage; 36 for they cannot even die anymore, because they are like angels, and <u>are sons of God, being sons of the resurrection.</u>”

Take note that this last passage in Luke 20 is stating that the sons of this age are the sons of God being sons of the resurrection. This passage states that the sons of this age marry and are given into marriage, not the angels. Think about the logic of Genesis 6. Does it make sense that fallen angels would take earthly wives, and instead of punishing the angels or the women that slept with them, God took it out on the men? No. What does the Scripture say? It says because of violence and because of the wickedness of man's heart that God was grieved that He made man.

Genesis 6:5-8 <u>Then the Lord saw that</u> **the wickedness of man** was great on the earth, and that <u>every intent of</u> **the thoughts of his heart** <u>was only evil continually</u>. 6 The Lord was <u>sorry</u> **that He had made man** on the earth, and He was grieved in His heart. 7 The Lord said, "<u>I will blot out</u> **man** whom I have created from the face of the land, from **man** <u>to animals to creeping things and to birds of the sky; for I am sorry that I have made them</u>." 8 But Noah found favor in the eyes of the Lord.

Men were continually walking contrary to the dominion of which they were supposed to govern. Because men refused to walk in the divinely set dominion that God had given, God exercised His dominion by removing man. They were evil. Paul mentions this sort in Romans 1:

Romans 1:28-32 And just as <u>they did not see fit to acknowledge God any longer</u>, God gave them over to a depraved mind, <u>to do those things which are not proper</u>, 29 being filled with all unrighteousness, wickedness, greed, evil; full of envy, murder, strife, deceit, malice; they are gossips, 30 slanderers, <u>haters of God,</u> insolent, arrogant, boastful, **inventors of evil**, disobedient to parents, 31 without understanding, untrustworthy, unloving, unmerciful; 32 and **although they know the ordinance of God**, that those who practice such things are worthy of death, **they not only do the same, but also give hearty approval to those who practice them**

2 Peter 2:5 ...and <u>did not spare the ancient world</u>, but

preserved Noah, a preacher of righteousness, with seven others, when He brought a flood upon the world of the **ungodly.**

God saved Noah because He was still walking in the created role. He was obedient to God and preaching God's righteousness to those who were engaging in all forms of sin. Think about this: God saw these men that bear His image and were created for His glory—created to be vessels of His love—and they were the *most* perverse, evil, hostile, violent, and lawless that people can be. Rapists, pedophiles, oppressors engaging in hedonistic, flesh-appeasing Darwinism. They lived by the mindset that if it feels good to the flesh, do it. If you want something, take it. If you're crossed, kill.

If the generational curses of breaking the eternal Law of God resulted in violent, incestuous men engaging in reproduction with members of their own family, then the violence that God saw grieved Him so much He destroyed mankind, sparing only Noah. These Nephilim were wiped out by the flood. God destroyed them all. So, why then do they reappear after the flood? We can see the answer to that in the text itself. In Genesis 9, when everyone gets off the boat, God reminds them:

> Genesis 9:6 "Whoever **sheds man's blood**, By man **his blood shall be shed**, For in the image of God He made man. 7"As for you, **be fruitful and multiply**; **Populate the earth** abundantly and **multiply** in it."

This is the third time God reminds mankind to be fruitful and multiply. In the garden, in the expulsion, and right after the destruction of the world. This is the contrast between the Nephilim destroyer and the

Righteous cultivator. What immediately happens after this catastrophic event of the world's destruction due to violence and rejection of God's ways? Ham and the issue of nakedness.

> Genesis 9:22-26 Ham, the father of Canaan, <u>saw the nakedness of his father</u>, and told his two brothers outside. 23 But Shem and Japheth took a garment and laid it upon both their shoulders and walked backward and <u>covered the nakedness of their father</u>; and their faces were turned away, so that <u>they did not see their father's nakedness</u>. 24 When Noah awoke from his wine, he knew what his youngest son had done to him. 25 So he said, <u>"Cursed be Canaan;</u> A servant of servants He shall be to his brothers." 26 He also said, "Blessed be the Lord, The God of Shem; And let Canaan be his servant.

This is gross, I know. In every way you look at it, I know it is gross, but let me show you from the Scriptures what I believe happened during this event, and why Noah cursed Ham's offspring instead of Ham. What does it mean to uncover nakedness in Leviticus 18?

> Leviticus 18:7-17 You shall not uncover <u>the nakedness of your father</u>, that is, <u>the nakedness of your mother.</u> She is your mother; you are not to uncover her nakedness. 8 You <u>shall not uncover the nakedness of your father's wife; it is your father's nakedness</u>. 9 The nakedness of your sister, either your father's daughter or your mother's daughter, whether born at home or born outside, their nakedness you shall not uncover. 10 The nakedness of your son's daughter or your daughter's daughter, their nakedness you shall not uncover; for their nakedness is

yours. 11 The nakedness of your father's wife's daughter, born to your father, she is your sister, you shall not uncover her nakedness. 12 You shall not uncover the nakedness of your father's sister; she is your father's blood relative. 13 You shall not uncover the nakedness of your mother's sister, for she is your mother's blood relative. 14 You shall not uncover the nakedness of your father's brother; you shall not approach his wife, she is your aunt. 15 You shall not uncover the nakedness of your daughter-in-law; she is your son's wife, you shall not uncover her nakedness. 16 You shall not uncover the nakedness of your brother's wife; it is your brother's nakedness. 17 <u>You shall not uncover the nakedness of a woman and of her daughter, nor shall you take her son's daughter or her daughter's daughter, to uncover her nakedness; they are blood relatives. It is lewdness</u>

Gross. It's in the Bible because people have struggled with it. The command is there for a reason. Here's the definition:

> (2) *wickedness, a wicked deed.* Psal. 26:10; 119:150. Especially used in speaking of sins of uncleanness, such as fornication, rape, or incest. Lev. 18:17, זִמָּה הִיא "this would be wickedness."

In Ham's case, it was to engage in incest and rape. How can we be sure? Because in the passage of Leviticus 18, it states that the inhabitants of *Cannan* did these very things.

Leviticus 18:1-3;26-27 Then the Lord spoke to Moses, saying, 2 "Speak to the sons of Israel and say to them, 'I am the Lord your God. 3 <u>You shall not do what is done in the land of Egypt</u> <u>where you lived, nor are you to do what is done in the land of</u> <u>Canaan</u> where I am bringing you; you shall not walk in their statutes.

26 But as for you, you are to keep My statutes and My judgments <u>and shall not do any of these abominations, neither</u> <u>the native, nor the alien</u> who sojourns among you 27 (for <u>the</u> <u>men of the land who have been before you have done all these</u> <u>abominations, and the land has become defiled)</u>

God destroyed the world filled with people who engaged in this lewdness, and then Noah and his sons were spared because of Noah's righteousness. Ham engaged in the same practices that destroyed the world before him, incest and rape and lewd acts of dominance.

It then makes sense as to why Noah curses the *son* of Ham. This son was the product of that incestuous rape of Ham's mother, as his father Noah lay vulnerable and unconscious from wine. It also explains the post-flood return of the Nephilim, as the practices of selective breeding and incest returned immediately. As men again sprawled out over the face of the earth and built cities, some in hostile defiance towards God, perhaps even angry that He wiped out the old, lewd ways. Some probably bore grudges against God. God created mankind for a purpose, and that purpose is contrary to our wicked, fleshly desires that are naturally hostile to His Spirit. Anak and Goliath, his descendant, were from the line of Canaan.

As the people populated the earth and men again began to engage in the practices of wickedness, and as the history of the dominance of the barbarian warlord type of man grew stronger, passed down from Noah's descendants, then it might explain why Abraham and Issac both were afraid as they sojourned in the foreign lands. If they knew that their wives were beautiful and they were familiar with the family history of men murdering godly people to steal their wives as their own, then it would be at the very least an understandable fear that drove them to tell their wives to pretend to be their sisters rather than their wives. The fear that a violent Nephilim man of dominance would murder them and take their beautiful wives as their own was valid. While this might just be a theory, it's a reasonable one that bears itself out in the context of these stories.

What we don't see, however, is the post-flood idea that post-heaven angels retained the title "sons of God" and sired another batch of half-angel, half-human giants. Here's a question to consider: Scripture states that God is the one who opens and closes the womb, and it also states that God is the one that knits together in the womb.

> Psalms 139:13-16 <u>For You formed my inward parts; You wove me in my mother's womb.</u> 14 I will give thanks to You, <u>for I am fearfully and wonderfully made; Wonderful are Your works</u>, And my soul knows it very well. 15 My frame was not hidden from You, When I was made in secret, And skillfully wrought in the depths of the earth; 16 <u>Your eyes have seen my unformed substance; And in Your book were all written The days that were ordained for me, When as yet there was not one of them.</u>

Genesis 30:17-22 <u>God gave heed</u> to Leah, and she conceived and bore Jacob a fifth son. 18 Then Leah said, "God has given me my wages because I gave my maid to my husband." So she named him Issachar. 19 <u>Leah conceived again</u> and bore a sixth son to Jacob. 20 Then Leah said, <u>"God has endowed me with a good gift</u>; now my husband will dwell with me, because I have borne him six sons." So she named him Zebulun. 21 Afterward she bore a daughter and named her Dinah. 22 <u>Then God remembered Rachel, and God gave heed to her and opened her womb.</u>

Acts 17:25 <u>The God who made the world and **all things in it,**</u> since He is Lord of heaven and earth, does not dwell in temples made with hands; 25 nor is He served by human hands, as though He needed anything, since **He Himself gives to all people life and breath and all things**

Romans 11:36 <u>For from Him and through Him and to Him are all things</u>. To Him be the glory forever. Amen.

As all life comes from God, and He is the one who opens and closes the womb, and He knits together life in the womb, then the logic of the fallen angel demon-baby theory becomes this: God rejected angels and kicked them out of heaven then allowed them to enter into sexual relationships with women of earth and procreate a new half-man, half-angel creature—and He allowed this by opening the wombs of these women and then knitting together these giant half-breed demi god-like creatures. Then He flooded the earth because of these same giant demon human babies. That is not good doctrine. That is foolishness. There are no verses that say angels are sons of God anywhere in Scripture unless the reader inserts it into the text based not on the Word of God but based on their own suppositions from outside the word of God. I'll walk you through those passages too.

Some say that Job references angels where it says in Job 1:

> Job 1:6 Now <u>there was a day when the sons of God came to present themselves before the Lord</u>, and Satan also came among them.

And again in chapter 2:

> Job 2:1 <u>Again, there was a day when the sons of God came to present themselves before the Lord</u>, and Satan also came among them to present himself before the Lord.

The fact that "sons of God" appeared before the Lord does not automatically mean that the sons of God are angels and there is nothing in the text to support that. What is more harmonious to the totality of scripture, in my opinion, is that the sons of God are the righteous and obedient men. If we look at Exodus 23, we see the command for the righteous men of God to appear before Him:

> Exodus 23:14-16 "<u>Three times a year you shall celebrate a feast to Me</u>. 15 You shall keep the Feast of Unleavened Bread; for seven days you are to eat unleavened bread, as I commanded you, at the appointed time in the month of Abib, for in that month you came out of Egypt. <u>And no one is to appear before</u>

Me empty-handed. 16 Also you shall keep the Feast of the Harvest of the first fruits of your labors from what you sow in the field; also the Feast of the Ingathering at the end of the year when you gather in the fruit of your labors from the field. 17 Three times a year all your males shall appear before the Lord God.

Echoed in Exodus 34:

Exodus 34: 19-24 "The firstborn from every womb belongs to Me, and all your male livestock, the firstborn from cattle and sheep. 20 You shall redeem with a lamb the firstborn from a donkey; and if you do not redeem it, then you shall break its neck. You shall redeem all the firstborn of your sons. None are to appear before Me empty-handed.

21 "You shall work six days, but on the seventh day you shall rest; even during plowing time and harvest you shall rest. 22 And you shall celebrate the Feast of Weeks, that is, the first fruits of the wheat harvest, and the Feast of Ingathering at the turn of the year. 23 Three times a year all your males are to appear before the Lord God, the God of Israel. 24 For I will drive out nations from you and enlarge your borders, and no one will covet your land when you go up three times a year to appear before the Lord your God.

Three times a year, all the righteous and obedient men are to appear before the Lord. Three times a year, we're to come to the Father and appear before the King. This is the Passover where God makes the distinction between those who are His and those who are in rebellion.

82

It's the beginning of the harvest when we are to be about the business that God created us to be about. And it is the end of the harvest when we rejoice with God that He may say well done good and faithful servant. As mentioned previously, Jethro was a Midianite priest and Job was a righteous man.

> Job 1:1 There was a man in the land of Uz whose name was Job; <u>and that man was blameless, upright, fearing God</u> and turning away from evil.

Job would fit under the definition of a son of God in light of the Scriptures mentioned previously. Interesting enough, Exodus 34 talks about protection for these men who appear before God:

> Exodus 34: 24 For <u>I will drive out nations before you</u> and enlarge your borders, and <u>no man shall covet your land</u> when <u>you go up three times a year to appear before the Lord your God</u>.

Is this not the very objection Satan makes to God that is applying to Job:

> Job 1: Have You not made <u>a fence around him and his house and all that he has</u>, on every side? <u>You have blessed the work of his hands, and his possessions have increased in the land.</u>

This protection of God as mentioned in Exodus and afforded to Job is the protection that Josephus remarks upon:

> " But what is here chiefly remarkable is this, that no foreign nation ever came thus to destroy the Jews at any of their

solemn festivals, from the days of Moses till this time, but came now upon their apostasy from God, and from obedience to him. Nor is it possible, in the nature of things, that in any other nation such vast numbers should be gotten together, and perish in the siege of any one city whatsoever, as now happened in Jerusalem." -Flavius Josephus, The Wars of the Jews William Whiston, A.M., Ed.

Job was a righteous man, and what did that man do?

Job 2:1 Again, there was a day when the sons of God came to present themselves before the Lord, and Satan also came among them to present himself before the Lord.
Job 2:3 The Lord said to Satan, "Have you considered My servant Job? For there is no one like him on the earth, a blameless and upright man fearing God and turning away from evil. And he still holds firm to his integrity, although you incited Me against him to ruin him without cause.

Look at what we see in this passage in 1 Samuel:

1 Samuel 1:21 Then the man Elkanah went up with all his household to offer to the Lord the yearly sacrifice and pay his vow. 22 But Hannah did not go up, for she said to her husband, "I will not go up until the child is weaned; then I will bring him, that he may appear before the Lord and stay there forever."

It's reasonable to see that Job was performing at least the annual sacrifices when the men are called to appear before God, and Job is concerned that his household hasn't done this. That suggests sons of God are a classification of people that do righteousness, and those who don't are not sons of God. This is affirmed in Scripture time and again.

> 1 John 3:10 No one who has been born of God practices sin, because His seed remains in him; and he cannot sin continually, because he has been born of God. 10 <u>By this the children of God and the children of the devil are obvious</u>: anyone who does not practice righteousness is not of God, nor the one who does not love his brother and sister.

Ergo, the men of righteousness appearing before the Lord at the appointed times would be in line with men, and not angels, being the sons of God. Those that hold to the fallen angel demon-baby theory point to Job 38 to say that this must mean angels. The case made by those who hold to this position is that the stars sing and they are angels who sing and because angels sing, they're also the sons of God. Using Job 38:7 to say that sons of God means angels is still an injection of that interpretation to the text when the text doesn't suppose it. This is what it says:

> Job 38:7 When <u>the morning stars sang together</u> And <u>all the sons of God shouted for joy</u>?

That was it. That verse doesn't say angels are the sons of God. It doesn't equate the two. It only says that these sons of God shouted for joy. Now, I grant that the context of this passage is God talking about the creation of the world. However, in this passage, we see creative imagery and not literal things. The sea is not enclosed with doors, and it didn't come from the womb. Clouds aren't clothes. Morning stars and sons of God shouting for joy doesn't mean that sons of God are angels.

If we consider Job 38 where God is communicating His deep concepts to Job and He mentions stars singing and sons of God, we still would have to inject angels as one of these two things in a poetic passage that also states that ice comes from "lady parts", as verse 29 states. This would also indicate that God wasn't down-dressing Job verbally, but that Job was actually at creation during its formation as God says, "tell me who laid the foundation because surely you were there".

> Job 38:19 "Where is the way to the dwelling of light? And darkness, where is its place,
> 20 That you may take it to its territory And that you may discern the paths to its home?
> 21 "You know, for you were born then, And the number of your days is great!

It's a hyper literalism fallacy. It's rhetorical. God is not reminding Job that Job was there when He created Adam and commanded the bounds of light and darkness. He's speaking in poetic imagery to remind Job that *God* is sovereign and beyond Jobs' understanding. Here's another thing to think about in relation to these "stars":

> Jude 1: 12 **These are the men** who are hidden reefs in your love feasts when they feast with you without fear, caring for themselves; clouds without water, carried along by winds;

86

autumn trees without fruit, doubly dead, uprooted; 13 wild waves of the sea, casting up their own shame like foam; **wandering stars,** for whom the black darkness has been reserved forever

Jude is calling these stars men. The context of Jude is a different disposition of the men as Job records a joyful, worshiping event, and Jude has those men as becoming rebellious and reserved for judgment—both still refer to men.

Let's also look at the contrast found in Psalms 148 where it appears that angels are a separate classification from both the sun and moon and even the stars that give praise, as well as these humans who praise Him:

Psalm 148 1-14 Praise the Lord! Praise the Lord from the heavens; Praise Him in the heights! 2 Praise Him, all His angels; Praise Him, all His heavenly armies! 3 Praise Him, sun and moon; Praise Him, all stars of light! 4 Praise Him, highest heavens, And the waters that are above the heavens! 5 They are to praise the name of the Lord, For He commanded and they were created. 6 He has also established them forever and ever; He has made a decree, and it will not pass away. 7 Praise the Lord from the earth, Sea monsters, and all the ocean depths; 8 Fire and hail, snow and clouds; Stormy wind, fulfilling His word; 9 Mountains and all hills; Fruit trees and all cedars; 10 Animals and all cattle; Crawling things and winged fowl; 11 Kings of the earth and all peoples; Rulers and all judges of the earth; 12 Both young men and virgins; Old men and children. 13 They are to praise the name of the Lord, For His name alone is exalted;

His majesty is above earth and heaven. 14 <u>And He has lifted up a horn for His people, Praise for all His godly ones, For the sons of Israel, a people near to Him. Praise the Lord!</u>

When some choose to read Job 38:7 as "stars singing next to sons of God shouting" as "because these are side-by-side and in the same event they *must* both be the same", we are obligated to reason the same manner to Psalm 148 and disregard all context and say that everything is angels. Sun, moon, angels, Israel, the sea, fire, hail, clouds, all of it is now angels. God goes into detail in telling us how He created everything in Genesis 1. He didn't mention making the angels at creation, so to inject that interpretation of angels into both Job 38:7 and Genesis 1 is taking heavy liberties in adding and subtracting scripture. (God did create angels according to Nehemiah 9:6, we just don't know when.,)

A critique of this explanation is that it must be grounded as a metaphor. Morning stars and sons of God at creation are speaking to a "thing" and are not metaphoric in and of themselves. A metaphor being grounded in reality is a fair criticism.

If it is not a metaphor, is there a text that places sons of God as men rather than the ascription to angels? For this, let us look back at Genesis.

Genesis 1:26-28 Then God said, "Let Us make <u>mankind</u> in Our image, according to Our likeness; and <u>let them</u> rule over the fish of the sea and over the birds of the sky and over the livestock and over all the earth, and over every crawling thing that crawls on the earth." 27 <u>So God created man</u> in His own image, in the image of God <u>He created him; male and female He created them.</u> 28 God blessed <u>them</u>; and <u>God said to them,</u>

"Be fruitful and multiply, and fill the earth, and subdue it; and rule over the fish of the sea and over the birds of the sky and over every living thing that moves on the earth."

During creation, mankind was made. Adam walked with God in the Garden and some believe that God was pre-incarnate Christ, Yeshua in the flesh. *If* Christ was in the flesh walking and praising the Father with Adam, then the sons of God would both be shouting for joy and that would satisfy Job 38, but let's look further in Genesis 5:

Genesis 5:1-2 This is the book of the generations of Adam. On the day when God created man, He made him in the likeness of God. 2 He created them male and female, and He blessed them and named them "mankind" on the day when they were created.

This is stating that on that day of creation, when God created man, He created *them* male and female. Mankind is made in the image of God. Mankind is plural. Them is plural. During creation, to some degree, Adam, the son of God (contained within himself a plurality), all future generations were within him. Him, shouting for joy in worship, is the reason mankind was created. We were created to reflect God's glory in His image. When Adam had a son, it says he made his son in the likeness of Adam. Part of Adam went out from within himself into the creation of his son. Contained within Adam at his creation was Eve and every seed for every son that would ever be. In this poetic sense, Adam was one, but many. If he praised God, all humanity praised God. The same language that is used for God making Adam is used for Adam making his son. Does Scripture say anywhere that angels were created in the image of God, that they may be called sons?

Scripture doesn't even mention angels in the Genesis chapter 1 or 2 creation accounts, so it would be more reasonable for it to be Adam. Adam is mentioned. Eve is mentioned. Mankind is mentioned. Angels are not. So, to take Job and put angels into verse 37 just doesn't fit. Luke 3:38 states that Adam was a son of God the same way Genesis 5 does through genealogy:

> Luke 3:38 the son of Enosh, the son of Seth, <u>the son of Adam, the son of God.</u>

Adam, in a pre-sin, perfect state, would be in perfect obedience to God and qualify as *both* definitions of sons of God. Furthermore, since Job 38 must have a grounding for its spring boarding, then let's take a look at the importance of Hebrews 1:

> Hebrews 1:5 For to which of the angels did He ever say,
> "<u>You are My Son</u>, Today I have fathered You"?
> And again, "<u>I will be a Father to Him</u>
> <u>And He will be a Son to Me</u>"?

Granted, this is about the Messiahship of the Savior, but this implies that God never said to angels, "you are My sons", as they are not sons of God but people are. If God had anywhere said this about angels, then the answer to the question posed when asked, "Of which of the angels did God ever say You are My Son?" would be "Steve, the angel son of God," or "Todd the angel, God's son". Since it is not the case, we have to ask ourselves, "Can we find a single example in Scripture where an angel is called a son? I haven't found one and believe me friends, I have been looking. Instead, we have examples of God calling men sons of God.

Job 1, and 2 are referencing the faithful, obedient men of God appearing before the Lord at the three appointed feasts. As it states in Exodus 23 and 34:

> Exodus 23:17 Three times a year all your males(sons) shall appear before the Lord God (God).
> Exodus 34 :23 Three times a year all your males (sons)are to appear before the Lord God, the God of Israel. 24 For I will drive out nations from you and enlarge your borders, and no one will covet your land when you go up three times a year to appear before the Lord your God.

Even if you didn't want to go with Adam being a singular man with all generations within him to account for the sons praising, or you didn't want to assume that Christ in the garden worshiping God might fit the passage, there is still another option. Noah. After God flooded the earth and destroyed the world everything that wasn't on the ark:

> Job 38:7-11 When the morning stars sang together
> And all the sons of God shouted for joy?
> 8 "Or who enclosed the sea with doors
> When, bursting forth, it went out from the womb;
> 9 When I made a cloud its garment
> And thick darkness its swaddling band,
> 10 And I placed boundaries on it
> And set a bolt and doors,

11 And I said, 'Thus far you shall come, but no farther;
And here shall your proud waves stop'?

Similar language is used that relates to the flood.

> Genesis 7:11-12 In the six hundredth year of Noah's life, in the second month, on the seventeenth day of the month, on the same day all the fountains of the great deep burst open, and the floodgates of the sky were opened. 12 The rain fell upon the earth for forty days and forty nights.

A case could be made that the language in Job references how God opened the earth and had the water rise, as well as made the clouds dark in torrential, downpouring rain, and it continued to fill the earth until God said stop. Did Noah worship God after he left the ark?

> Genesis 8 :18-20 So Noah went out, and his sons and his wife and his sons' wives with him. 19 Every beast, every creeping thing, and every bird, everything that moves on the earth, went out by their families from the ark. 20 Then Noah built an altar to the Lord, and took of every clean animal and of every clean bird and offered burnt offerings on the altar.

He did. That gives us three reasonable explanations of who these sons of God are without injecting angels into the text and distorting other texts.

Critics of these reasonable explanations of who the sons of God are tend to get hung up on the language used for the term. In most places, the phrase is "*beni Elohim,*" which means sons of God. In a few places it says "*beni ha Elohim,*" which means...sons of God. They argue that there is a special designation for "*beni ha Elohim*" that must mean angels are literal sons of God. This is an argument from silence, because even if there is a differing qualifier to emphasize specific sonship, there is no verse that tells us that this is referring to the angels. Rather, Adam is a son of God. He has no father but God. Adam is not an angelic being, even though he fits the definition of being a literal son of God. Genesis 5 and Luke 3 both designate that Adam is a son of God.

> Genesis 5:1 This is the book of the generations of Adam. <u>In the day when God created man, He made him</u> in the likeness of God.

> Luke 3:38 the son of Enosh, the son of Seth, <u>the son of Adam, the son of God.</u>

In the obedient sense, we become grafted-in sons of God. In the literal sense by creation, God is our Father.

> Malachi 2:10 <u>"Do we not all have one father?</u> Has not one <u>God created us?</u> Why do we deal treacherously each against his brother so as to profane the covenant of our fathers?

Both designations "*beni Elohim*" and "*beni ha Elohim*" are accounted for without needing to push other Scriptures out of their place to hammer together a fallen, demon-giant baby scenario.

In summary, sons of God aren't angels falling and taking earthly wives and making giant babies. Nor are the sons of God just a specific line of Seth or based on heredity at all. Walking in God's ways are what it means to be adopted sons of God, grafted into His house through obedience and love for Him.

CHAPTER SIX

Jude

Jude is a powerhouse of context in a book that is only a page. Jude gives us insight and direction concerning some early church matters. Having established what the sons of God are, and what the Nephlim are, we should be able to read Jude without external, non-canonical texts distorting the Scriptures. The matter concerning Jude doesn't appear to be that angels were kicked out of Heaven for wanting sex with women, but rather, it is about those who were infiltrating the church from the Judaizers trying to implement Rabbinic law and preventing Gentiles from obeying God's Law. It's about men who are trying to subjugate the gentiles turning to faith and subject them to traditions instead of Christ. While angels are used in an example regarding not trusting in a position, surrounding, or your own strength, but rather, in the assurance and power of God's authority, Jude is not about angels. Jude is about walking in submission to God's dominion rather than self-will and the faulty, misleading power of the flesh. Let's look at how Jude (the brother of Christ by the way, fun fact) starts his letter and what he's addressing.

> Jude 1:1-4 Beloved, while I was making every effort to write
> you about our common salvation, I felt the necessity to write
> to you appealing that you contend earnestly for the faith which
> was once for all handed down to the saints. 4 **For certain**
> **persons have crept in unnoticed**, those who were long

beforehand marked out for this condemnation, **ungodly persons** who turn the grace of our God into licentiousness and deny our only Master and Lord, Jesus Christ.

Every time I read this introduction, what I see is Jude who is writing to warn against men who are distorting and twisting the truth about God's gift of grace bringing salvation through Christ. The particular angle of their distortion is promoting license to sin and deny the ways of Christ our Master—denying the dominion and rulership of Christ. How does the text go from "There are bad actors infiltrating our church, teaching people to deny God" to "We must look outside of Scriptures for prophecies and allow non-biblical books to interpret what the Scriptures mean"? The examples set out in Jude that get distorted are:

- Believers, saved from Egypt—and Egyptians destroyed
- Angels , removed from heaven—to place of destruction
- Sodom and Gomorrah—place of destruction. like surrounding cities, going to places of destruction.

The emphasis being not to compromise from obedience and walking in God's righteous directives to following after fleshly assurances like lusts. The lust of the flesh is not only about sexual lusts and sin. There is no reason to be hyperfocal on sexual sin when the passage is about not succumbing to any of the fleshly lusts. That can include overindulging and eating things that are not food, according to God. That can include harboring malice. The word for desire or "lusts of the flesh" are Strong's G1939. The same word used here:

Luke 22:15 And He said to them, "I have eagerly desired **G1939** to eat this Passover with you before I suffer

As well as:

Philippians 1:23 But I am hard-pressed from both directions, having the desire **G1939** to depart and be with Christ, for that is very much better

This isn't some sexual perversion in wanting to keep the Passover. That is not a freaky sex thing that Paul is suggesting. It would be wrong to promote such a view. Don't do that. Don't be gross like that.

Let's look at the Jude passage as it reads from 2 Peter:

2 Peter 2:4-5 For if God did not spare angels when they sinned, but cast them into hell and committed them to pits of darkness, held for judgment; 5 and did not spare the ancient world, but protected Noah, a preacher of righteousness, with seven others, when He brought a flood upon the world of the ungodly; 6 and if He condemned the cities of Sodom and Gomorrah to destruction by reducing them to ashes, **having made them an example of what is coming for the ungodly**; 7 and if He rescued righteous Lot, who was oppressed by the perverted conduct of unscrupulous people 8 (for by what he saw and heard that righteous man, while living among them, felt his righteous soul tormented day after day by their lawless deeds), 9 then the Lord knows how to rescue the

godly from **a trial,** and to keep the unrighteous under
punishment for the day of judgment,

Note that the passages in Jude and Peter are practically the same; the
emphasis is about not losing a place of security for a place of destruction.
Also, again, an important highlight is verse 4:

> For if God did not spare angels when they sinned, but cast
> them into hell and committed them to pits of darkness, held
> for judgment...

Hell, darkness, held for judgment...none of that leaves room for taking
human wives. What is Jude talking about? Let's walk through it
together.

> Jude 1:3-4 Beloved, while I was making every effort to write
> you about our common salvation, I felt the necessity to write
> to you appealing that you contend earnestly for the faith which
> was once for all handed down to the saints 4 For certain people
> have crept in unnoticed, those who were long beforehand
> marked out for this condemnation, ungodly persons who turn
> the grace of our God into indecent behavior and deny our only
> Master and Lord, Jesus Christ.

People who appear to be of Salvation are trusting that they are secure
and are actually marked for destruction. This is used as an example in
several following verses. Note the context is those who presume to be
secure, and are then destroyed.

Jude 1:5 Now I want to remind you, though you know everything once and for all, that the Lord, **after** saving a people out of the land of Egypt, **subsequently** destroyed those who did not believe.

Taken from a place—Egypt
Then—Destroyed

There were those who trusted in themselves and became arrogant. Korah rebelled against God and Moses' authority AFTER being redeemed from Egypt and the plagues that brought judgment. Of note is that in this following verse, it is the only place angels are mentioned, whereas translators add the word angels in two other verses to "reconstruct the meaning of the text" to be a doctrine regarding angels rather than about those who are putting trust in something other than God and following through with faith obedience.

Jude 1:6 And angels who did not keep their own domain but abandoned their proper dwelling place, these He has kept in eternal restraints under darkness for the judgment of the great day

Angels had a place—Heaven
Then—Chained in darkness for judgment day

Jude 1:7 just as Sodom and Gomorrah and the cities around them, since they in the same way as these indulged in sexual perversion and went after strange flesh, are exhibited as an

<u>example in undergoing the punishment</u> of eternal fire.- Jude

A secure place—Sodom and Gomorrah
Then—like the cities surrounding were destroyed for sexual deviance

People try to take verses 6, 7, and 8 to be speaking about angels falling and engaging in sex, presumably to try and build a case for fallen angels being sons of God and drawing off of the extrabiblical Enoch text. There is a huge problem with this: the words angels and angelic aren't in verses 7 and 8. As is done with other passages like Job, assumptions are made and then doctrines are built upon them. Jude states that the angels are in darkness awaiting judgment day, Enoch says that they are cast to earth, develop genitals, enter into covenant relationships with earth women rather than simply fornicate, and sire a race of half-angel, half-human breed of giants. They shoehorn this mindset into the text to make it say something to affirm that doctrine rather than what the text bears out.

Jude 1:8-10 <u>Yet in the same way</u> **these people** <u>also, dreaming,</u> **defile the flesh**, reject authority**, and speak abusively** of majesties. 9 But Michael the archangel, when he disputed with the devil and argued about the body of Moses, <u>did not dare pronounce against him an abusive judgment</u>, but said, "The Lord rebuke you!" 10 **But these people** <u>disparage all the things that they do not understand; and all the things that they know by instinct, like unreasoning animals,</u> by these things they are destroyed.

Again the context is having a reverence for God and not a debased fleshly assurance or levying slander. Rather than this being an extrabiblical showdown of the angels and the Devil, of which we would have to look elsewhere than the Scripture to find, I find that the reasoned explanation is that the body of Moses in question is not the physical bones of the Prophet, but rather a reference to the church and the argument with Joshua the High priest.

> Zechariah 3:1-5 Then he showed me Joshua the high priest standing before the angel of the Lord, and Satan standing at his right to accuse him. 2 And the Lord said to Satan, "The Lord rebuke you, Satan! Indeed, the Lord who has chosen Jerusalem rebuke you! Is this not a log snatched from the fire?" 3 Now Joshua was clothed in filthy garments and was standing before the angel. 4 And he responded and said to those who were standing before him, saying, "Remove the filthy garments from him." Again he said to him, "See, I have taken your guilt away from you and will clothe you with festive robes." 5 Then I said, "Have them put a clean headband on his head." So they put the clean headband on his head and clothed him with garments, while the angel of the Lord was standing by.

He continues to say that in obedience, faithfulness leads to being a member of the house of God.

> Zechariah 3:6-7 And the angel of the Lord admonished Joshua, saying, 7 "The Lord of armies says this: 'If you walk in My ways **and perform My service**, then you will both govern

My house and be in charge of My courtyards, and I will grant you free access among these who are standing here.

It's about Joshua accepting the position of High Priest in humility and submission to God. Note that this interpretation, without sensationalism, now fits not only within the bounds of established Scripture but also fits within the context of Jude in that it is about humbly serving God and that faithfulness will be rewarded *instead* of spewing slander against others and turning aside to the works of the flesh.

> Jude1:11-13 Woe to them! For they have gone the way of Cain, and for pay they have given themselves up to the error of Balaam, and perished in the rebellion of Korah. 12 These are the ones who are hidden reefs in your love feasts when they feast with you without fear, like shepherds caring only for themselves; clouds without water, carried along by winds; autumn trees without fruit, doubly dead, uprooted; 13 wild waves of the sea, churning up their own shameful deeds like dirty foam; wandering stars, for whom the gloom of darkness has been reserved forever.

Who was Cain? He was a man who was offering sacrifices to God and was warned by God that sin was looking to rule over him, but he must master it. Just like the context of these men in Jude that they must not trust in anything except God, rather continuing in faithfulness, not trusting in self or position or place or even manmade doctrine. Now let's look at an objection regarding a prophecy that people say is quoting from extrabiblical sources such as Enoch:

Jude 1:14-15 It was also about these men that Enoch, in the seventh generation from Adam, prophesied, saying, "Behold, the Lord came with many thousands of His holy ones, 15 to execute judgment upon all, and to convict all the ungodly of all their ungodly deeds which they have done in an ungodly way, and of all the harsh things which ungodly sinners have spoken against Him."

- the Lord
- with Holy Ones
- and to repay the ungodly of their deeds

Matthew 16:27 For the Son of Man is going to come in the glory of His Father with His angels, and **WILL THEN REPAY EVERY PERSON ACCORDING TO HIS DEEDS.**

- The Lord
- with Holy Ones
- and to repay the ungodly of their deeds

Psalms 149:4-9 For the Lord takes pleasure in His people; He will beautify the afflicted ones with salvation. 5 Let the godly ones exult in glory; Let them sing for joy on their beds. 6 Let the high praises of God be in their mouth, and a two-edged sword in their hand, 7 To execute vengeance on the nations And punishment on the peoples, 8 To bind their kings with chains And their nobles with fetters of iron, 9 To execute on them the judgment written; This is an honor for all His godly ones. Praise the Lord!

- The Lord
- with Holy Ones
- and to repay the ungodly of their deeds

Matthew 25:31-34;40-46 But when the Son of Man comes in His glory, and all the angels with Him, then He will sit on His glorious throne. 32 All the nations will be gathered before Him; and He will separate them from one another, as the shepherd separates the sheep from the goats; 33 and He will put the sheep on His right, and the goats on the left.34 "Then the King will say to those on His right, 'Come, you who are blessed of My Father, inherit the kingdom prepared for you from the foundation of the world.... 40 The King will answer and say to them, 'Truly I say to you, to the extent that you did it to one of these brothers of Mine, even the least of them, you did it to Me.' 41 "Then He will also say to those on His left, 'Depart from Me, accursed ones, into the eternal fire which has been prepared for the devil and his angels; ... 44 Then they themselves also will answer, 'Lord, when did we see You hungry, or thirsty, or a stranger, or naked, or sick, or in prison, and did not take care of You?' 45 Then He will answer them, 'Truly I say to you, to the extent that you did not do it to one of the least of these, you did not do it to Me.' 46 These will go away into eternal punishment, but the righteous into eternal life."

- The Lord
- with Holy Ones
- and to repay the ungodly of their deeds

2 Thessalonians 1:5-9 This is a plain indication of God's righteous judgment so that you will be considered worthy of the kingdom of God, for which indeed you are suffering. 6 <u>For after all it is only just for</u> **God** <u>to</u> **repay with affliction** <u>those who afflict you</u>, 7 and to give relief to you who are afflicted and to us as well <u>when the</u> **Lord Jesus** <u>will be revealed from heaven with</u> **His mighty angels in flaming fire, 8 dealing out retribution** to **those who do not know God and to those who do not obey the gospel** of our Lord Jesus. 9 **These will pay the penalty of eternal destruction**, <u>away from the presence of the Lord and from the glory of His power</u>, 10 when **He comes to be glorified in His saints** <u>on that day, and to be marveled at among all who have believed— for our testimony to you was believed.</u>

- the Lord
- with Holy Ones
- and to repay the ungodly of their deeds

As seen here, the Jude prophecy is found in Scripture repeatedly without drawing from texts like Enoch. Even if Enoch were being used, it doesn't mean that Christ or Jude thought that Enoch was Scripture any more than Paul citing pagan philosophers and poets to convey a utilitarian truth.

Pagan authors quoted or alluded to are:

- Menander, Thais 218, quoting Euripides, "Evil company corrupts good habits" (1 Corinthians 15:33)
- Epimenides, de Oraculis, (Titus 1–12:13) where Paul introduces Epimenides as "a prophet of the Cretans"; see Epimenides paradox)
- Aratus, Phaenomena 5, (Acts 17:28 where Paul refers to the words of "some of your own poets")

None of these are Scripture or are considered Scripture and it would be wrong to do so.

Acts 17 : 24-28 The God who made the world and all things in it, since He is Lord of heaven and earth, does not dwell in temples made with hands; 25 nor is He served by human hands, as though He needed anything, since He Himself gives to all people life and breath and all things; 26 and He made from one man every nation of mankind to live on all the face of the earth, having determined their appointed times and the boundaries of their habitation, 27 that they would seek God, if perhaps they might grope for Him and find Him, though He is not far from each one of us; 28 <u>for in Him we live and move and exist, as even some of your own poets have said, 'For we also are His children.'</u> 29 **Being then the children of God**, we ought not to think that the Divine Nature is like gold or silver or stone, an image formed by the art and thought of man. 30 Therefore having overlooked the times of ignorance, <u>God is now declaring to men that all people everywhere should</u>

repent, 31 because **He has fixed a day in which He will judge the world in righteousness through a Man whom He has appointed, having furnished proof to all men by raising Him from the dead.**"

Returning back to Jude, we can see that Jude mentions Michael rebuking Satan. Some try to say that this is a reference to the external book of Enoch, but this is quite likely referencing Zechariah in context with the mentioning of the garments, the Angel of the Lord, and Joshua.

Jude 1:8-9 Yet in the same way these men, also by dreaming, defile the flesh, and reject authority, and revile angelic majesties. 9 **But Michael the archangel, when he disputed with the devil** and argued about the body of Moses, did not dare pronounce against him a railing judgment, but said, "**The Lord rebuke you!**"

Jude 1:18-23 But you, beloved, ought to remember the words that were spoken beforehand by the apostles of our Lord Jesus Christ, 18 that they were saying to you, "In the last time there will be mockers, following after their own ungodly lusts." 19 These are the ones who cause divisions, worldly-minded, devoid of the Spirit. 20 But you, beloved, building yourselves up on your most holy faith, praying in the Holy Spirit, 21 keep yourselves in the love of God, looking forward to the mercy of our Lord Jesus Christ to eternal life. 22 And have mercy on some, who are doubting; 23 **save others, snatching them out of the fire;** and on some have mercy with fear, **hating even the garment polluted by the flesh**.

Let's see the parallels in the passage with Zechariah and the unclean garment, and giving the clean

> Zechariah 3:2-5 2 The Lord said to Satan, "**The Lord rebuke you**, Satan! Indeed, the Lord who has chosen Jerusalem rebuke you! **Is this not a brand plucked from the fire**?" 3 Now Joshua was clothed with **filthy garments** and standing before the angel. "See, I have taken your guilt away from you and will clothe you with festive robes." 5 Then I said, "Have them put a clean headband on his head." So they put the clean headband on his head and clothed him with garments, while the angel of the Lord was standing by

Joshua before Satan—both passages
The Angel of the Lord—both passages
Being plucked from the fire—both passages
Accusations being made against the people of God—both passages
Garments polluted by flesh—both passages

The Zechariah passage is about Joshua who was appointed to take over as the High Priest and leader of Israel, as well as those with Joshua as priests. The priests were to not have dirty priestly garments and appear before the Lord, but God gave Joshua clean garments. Just as Satan was standing before Joshua to accuse him of breaking the Law of God by having dirty garments, so too were these infiltrators who had crept into the church trying to accuse true believers and lead them away from obedience. That is why Jude makes this parallel that just as Joshua didn't respond from a flesh-based, self-righteous justification to argue with Satan; rather, he called on the Lord to rebuke Satan, *so too* should the men call on God to remove those who are in the church who were appearing before Him with unwashed robes and walking in defilement.

In conclusion, Jude is not about angel sex or quoting a prophecy from an external source; it's about our security not being in a place, a doctrine, ourselves, or our flesh. It is found in Christ alone and we must be faithful and humble that He clothed us in Him and His righteousness.

> Jude 1:24 Now to Him who is able to protect you from stumbling, and to make you stand in the presence of His glory, blameless with great joy, 25 to the only God our Savior, through Jesus Christ our Lord, be glory, majesty, **dominion**, and authority before all time and now and forever. Amen.

Jude makes it clear that he is speaking of people and the church:

> Jude 1:1-4 Beloved, while I was making every effort to write you about our common salvation, I felt the necessity to write to you appealing that you contend earnestly for the faith which was once for all handed down to the saints. 4 For certain persons have crept in unnoticed, those who were long beforehand marked out for this condemnation, ungodly persons who turn the grace of our God into licentiousness and deny our only Master and Lord, Jesus Christ.

Jude is encouraging people to return to the headship and leading of God in His dominion, just like Joshua. Jude mentions those who crept in. Who are they and what is their role in the church when discussing the people of God?

CHAPTER SEVEN

The Judaizer Controversy

If the Gospel of Christ is "Sinners can repent from their sins and be reconciled to God through faith in Christ," then what would a false Gospel be? Throughout time, since the Garden God has been saying that we are to be fruitful and multiply and walk with Him in His ways. We have rebelled against His Laws and His Holiness. If the Gospel is that we can cease from that rebellion, what is the false gospel that Paul writes about?

Galatians 1:6-7 I am amazed that you are so quickly <u>deserting Him who called you</u> by the grace of Christ<u>, for a different gospel</u>; 7 which is really not another; only <u>there are some who are disturbing you</u> and want to distort the gospel of Christ

Galatians 2:1-4 Then after an interval of fourteen years I went up again to Jerusalem with Barnabas, taking Titus along also. 2 <u>It was because of a revelation that I went up; and I submitted to them the gospel which I preach among the Gentiles, but I did so in private to those who were of reputation, for fear that I might be running, or had run, in vain.</u> 3 But not even Titus, who was with me, though he was a Greek, was compelled to be circumcised. 4 <u>But it was because of the false brethren secretly</u>

brought in, who had sneaked in to spy out our liberty which we have in Christ Jesus, in order to bring us into bondage-

What is this disturbance, what is this different Gospel that the entirety of Galatians was written to combat? What Galatians is: a rebuke to the pharisaic oral law, rabbinic customs, and those that preach that *in order to be saved*, one must *commit* a physical action or tradition and conversion to the teachings of rabbinic authority. What Galatians is not: a rebuke to those who are obeying God's Law.

> 1 Thessalonians 2:14 For you, brethren, became imitators of the churches of God in Christ Jesus that are in Judea, for you also endured the same sufferings at the hands of your own countrymen, even as they did from the Jews, 15 who both killed the Lord Jesus and the prophets, and drove us out. They are not pleasing to God, but hostile to all men, 16 hindering us from speaking to the Gentiles so that they may be saved; with the result that they always fill up the measure of their sins. But wrath has come upon them to the utmost.

> Acts 21:27-29 When the seven days were almost over, the Jews from Asia, upon seeing him in the temple, began to stir up all the crowd and laid hands on him, 28 crying out, "Men of Israel, come to our aid! This is the man who preaches to all men everywhere against our people and the law and this place; and besides he has even brought Greeks into the temple and has defiled this holy place." 29 For they had previously seen Trophimus the Ephesian in the city with him, and they supposed that Paul had brought him into the temple.

To understand what is happening in Acts 10 and 15, we must understand that there was a group of Jews and Pharisees who were infiltrating what was known as the Way, trying to stop the preaching to gentiles. Rabbinic law and tradition regarded gentiles as unclean. Peter, who perhaps had mental and emotional baggage with how people perceived him after his denial of Christ three times during the night of the crucifixion, was being carried away by the influence of these men as Paul states in the book of Galatians:

> Galatians 2:11-14 But when Cephas came to Antioch, I opposed him to his face, because he stood condemned. 12 For prior to the coming of certain men from James, he used to eat with the Gentiles; but when they came, he began to withdraw and hold himself aloof, fearing the party of the circumcision. 13 The rest of the Jews joined him in hypocrisy, with the result that even Barnabas was carried away by their hypocrisy. 14 But when I saw that they were not straightforward about the truth of the gospel, I said to Cephas in the presence of all, "If you, being a Jew, live like the Gentiles and not like the Jews, how is it that you compel the Gentiles to live like Jews?

Not like Christ, not in obedience to God's Law, but like these Jews who were regarding rabbinical authority instead of the Law of God. Peter is being rebuked for participation with this group that is regarding Gentiles as unclean and compelling them to obey rabbinic law. Before we get into Acts 10, there is context needed for Peter's vision. We must first look at the prophecy in Isaiah 56 concerning gentiles.

> Isaiah 56:6-11 Let not the foreigner who has joined himself to the Lord say, "The Lord will surely separate me from His

people." Nor let the eunuch say, "Behold, I am a dry tree." Also the foreigners who join themselves to the Lord, To minister to Him, and to love the name of the Lord, To be His servants, every one who keeps from profaning the sabbath And holds fast My covenant; 7 Even those I will bring to My holy mountain And make them joyful in My house of prayer. Their burnt offerings and their sacrifices will be acceptable on My altar; For My house will be called a house of prayer for all the peoples." 8 The Lord God, who gathers the dispersed of Israel, declares, "Yet others I will gather to them, to those already gathered."

9 All you beasts of the field, All you beasts in the forest, Come to eat.

10 His watchmen are blind, All of them know nothing. All of them are mute dogs unable to bark, Dreamers lying down, who love to slumber; 11 And the dogs are greedy, they are not satisfied. And they are shepherds who have no understanding; They have all turned to their own way, Each one to his unjust gain, to the last one.

This states outright that gentiles are supposed to be holding to the Law of God, keeping the Sabbath, and that they are the dispersed of Israel that will be gathered to those already gathered.

Matthew 15:24 But He answered and said, "I was sent only to the lost sheep of the house of Israel.

Christ said that to a gentile woman.

Phil 3:2-3 <u>Beware of the dogs, beware of the evil workers,</u>
<u>beware of the false circumcision</u>; 3 for we are the true
circumcision, who worship in the Spirit of God and glory in
Christ Jesus and <u>put no confidence in the flesh</u>

Paul says that those who are teaching that gentiles need to undergo
rabbinic ritual physical circumcision and convert to Pharisaic authority
are dogs, blind guides who have turned to their own way. Now with the
understanding of Isaiah 56 and Christ joining gentiles who are worried
about being separated from being Israel, we can understand Acts 10,
starting with the gentile Cornelius of the Italian Cohort.

Acts 10:1-8 Now there was a man at Caesarea named
Cornelius, <u>a centurion of what was called the Italian cohort</u>, 2
a devout man and <u>one who feared God with all his household</u>,
and gave many alms to the Jewish people and prayed to God
continually. 3 About the ninth hour of the day he clearly saw
in a vision an angel of God who had just come in and said to
him, "Cornelius!" 4 And fixing his gaze on him and being
much alarmed, he said, "What is it, Lord?" And he said to him,
<u>"Your prayers and alms have ascended as a memorial before</u>
<u>God.</u> 5 Now dispatch some men to Joppa and send for a man
named Simon, who is also called Peter; 6 he is staying with a
tanner named Simon, whose house is by the sea." 7 When the
angel who was speaking to him had left, he summoned two of
his servants and a devout soldier of those who were his
personal attendants, 8 and after he had explained everything to
them, he sent them to Joppa.

A gentile who has a memorial before God by his faith and his faithfulness is given a message from the Lord to summon Peter who, at this time, is being carried away with the hypocrisy of those men who were regarding gentiles as unclean and separating from them.

> Acts 10:9-16 On the next day, as they were on their way and approaching the city, Peter went up on the housetop about the sixth hour to pray. 10 But he became hungry and was desiring to eat; but while they were making preparations, he fell into a trance; 11 and he *saw the sky opened up, and an object like a great sheet coming down, lowered by four corners to the ground, 12 and there were in it all kinds of four-footed animals and crawling creatures of the earth and birds of the air. 13 A voice came to him, "Get up, Peter, kill and eat!" 14 But Peter said, "By no means, Lord, for I have never eaten anything unholy and unclean." 15 Again a voice came to him a second time, "What God has cleansed, no longer consider unholy." 16 This happened three times, and immediately the object was taken up into the sky.

Gentiles are approaching at the hour Peter would be withdrawing from Gentiles to eat, as they were making preparations before eating. Peter, who is supposed to be a shepherd and a watchman. Peter, who has been blind, was regarding the gentiles that Christ came for as separate from God, despite what Isaiah 56 says. Peter was supposed to be feeding gentiles as part of his commission from the Savior to feed His sheep. God didn't regard the gentiles as unclean because they are saved by grace through faith in the word of Christ just as everyone who has ever been saved has been saved.

Acts 10:17-19 Now while Peter was <u>greatly perplexed in mind</u>
<u>as to what the vision which he had seen might be</u>, behold, the
men who had been sent by Cornelius, having asked directions
for Simon's house, appeared at the gate; 18 and calling out,
they were asking whether Simon, who was also called Peter,
was staying there. 19 <u>While Peter was reflecting on the vision,</u>
<u>the Spirit said to him, "Behold, three men are looking for you.</u>

Peter, confused by the vision that he knew wasn't about our unchanging
God changing His irrevocable word and altering what He says is Holy
and what is abomination in regards to what we eat.

Acts 10:22-23 They said, "Cornelius, a centurion, <u>a righteous</u>
<u>and God-fearing man</u> well spoken of by the entire nation of the
Jews, was divinely directed by a holy angel to send for you to
come to his house and hear a message from you." 23 <u>So he</u>
<u>invited them in and gave them lodging.</u>

This is against rabbinic law.

Acts 10:23-29 And on the next day he got up and went away
with them, and some of the brethren from Joppa accompanied
him. 24 On the following day he entered Caesarea. <u>Now</u>
<u>Cornelius was waiting for them and had called together his</u>
<u>relatives and close friends.</u> 25 When Peter entered, Cornelius
met him, and fell at his feet and worshiped him. 26 But Peter
raised him up, saying, "Stand up; I too am just a man." 27 As
he talked with him, he entered and *found many people
assembled. 28 And he said to them, <u>"You yourselves know how</u>
<u>unlawful it is for a man who is a Jew to associate with a</u>
<u>foreigner or to visit him</u>; and yet <u>God has shown me that I</u>

should not call any man unholy or unclean. <u>29 That is why I came without even raising any objection when I was sent for.</u> So I ask for what reason you have sent for me.

Peter is met with a large gathering of gentiles. He entered their home and even stated that this is a violation of rabbinic law, stating that God's Law has no such prohibition. Peter came without reservation because the vision he was given was exclusively about gentiles.

Acts 10: 34-36 Opening his mouth, Peter said: "<u>I most certainly understand now that God is not one to show partiality,</u> 35 bu<u>t in every nation the man who fears Him and does what is right is welcome to Him.</u> 36 The word which He sent to the sons of Israel, preaching peace through Jesus Christ (He is Lord of all)—

Every nation, not just Jews.

Acts 10:44-48 While Peter was still speaking these words, the Holy Spirit fell upon all those who were listening to the message. 45 <u>All the circumcised believers who came with Peter were amazed, because the gift of the Holy Spirit had been poured out on the Gentiles also.</u>46 For they were hearing them speaking with tongues and exalting God. Then Peter answered, 47 "<u>Surely no one can refuse the water for these to be baptized who have received the Holy Spirit just as we did, can he</u>?" 48 And he ordered them to be baptized in the name of Jesus Christ. <u>Then they asked him to stay on for a few days.</u>

God grafts gentiles into Israel. They are saved. Peter says no one should object to these gentiles being baptized and he stayed in the house of the gentiles for a few days—against rabbinic authority.

> Acts 11:1-3 Now the apostles and the brethren who were throughout Judea heard that the Gentiles also had received the word of God. 2 And when Peter came up to Jerusalem, those who were circumcised took issue with him, 3 saying, "You went to uncircumcised men and ate with them."

The circumcision in Judea took issue with Peter not obeying rabbinic law against eating and entering the homes of gentiles/ uncircumcised men. Peter recounts to them that the vision was about including the gentiles in salvation.

> Acts 11:8 When they heard this, they quieted down and glorified God, saying, "Well then, God has granted to the Gentiles also the repentance that leads to life."

Which now brings us to Acts 15 and those men of the circumcision in Judea.

> Acts 15:1 Some men came down from Judea and began teaching the brethren, "Unless you are circumcised according to the custom of Moses, you cannot be saved.

> Acts 15:5 But some of the sect of the Pharisees who had believed stood up, saying, "It is necessary to circumcise them and to direct them to observe the Law of Moses."

Peter, having received correction by means of the vision and from Paul, stands up to those men.

> Acts 15:6-11 The apostles and the elders came together to look into this matter. 7 After there had been much debate, Peter stood up and said to them, "Brethren, you know that in the early days God made a choice among you, that by my mouth the Gentiles would hear the word of the gospel and believe. 8 And God, who knows the heart, testified to them giving them the Holy Spirit, just as He also did to us; 9 and He made no distinction between us and them, cleansing their hearts by faith. 10 Now therefore why do you put God to the test by placing upon the neck of the disciples a yoke which neither our fathers nor we have been able to bear? 11 But we believe that we are saved through the grace of the Lord Jesus, in the same way as they also are."

Peter rebukes the idea that one must ritually convert to rabbinic authority and engage in circumcision for the sake of being saved. We are not now, nor has anyone ever been, saved by works or by circumcision. Not in the Old Testament or the New Testament, but that group in Judea was teaching these manmade traditions for salvation. These burdensome traditions are what is spoken against in multiple places of which people make the faulty assumption that the passage is talking about God's Law when it is referring to the troubling rabbinic pharisaic law. They agreed that the gentiles shouldn't be under the charge to follow the Law to be saved and decided to give them four introductory, necessary commands from the Law of God, knowing that they would come every Sabbath and learn the rest of the Law.

Acts 15:19-21 Therefore it is my judgment that we do not trouble those who are turning to God from among the Gentiles, 20 but that we write to them that they abstain from things contaminated by idols and from fornication and from what is strangled and from blood. 21 <u>For Moses from ancient generations has in every city those who preach him, since he is read in the synagogues every Sabbath.</u>"

Moses here is an idiom for the commands of God. We know this is an introductory command because the Pharisees and the rabbinical authorities accused Paul of telling people to not obey God's commands, so much that Paul performed a Nazarite vow just to prove those rumors untrue:

Acts 21:17-24 After <u>we arrived in Jerusalem, the brethren received us gladly.</u> 18 And the following day <u>Paul went in with us to James, and all the elders were present.</u> 19 After he had greeted them, he began to relate o<u>ne by one the things which God had done among the Gentiles through his ministry.</u> 20 And when they heard it they began glorifying God; and they said to him, "<u>You see, brother, how many thousands there are among the Jews of those who have believed, and they are all zealous for the Law;</u> 21 and they have been told about you, that you are teaching all the Jews who are among the Gentiles to forsake Moses, telling them not to circumcise their children nor to walk according to the customs. 22 What, then, is to be done? They will certainly hear that you have come. 23 Therefore do this that we tell you. We have four men who are under a vow; 24 take them and purify yourself along with them, and pay their expenses so that they may shave their heads; <u>and all will know that there is nothing to the things which they have been told about you, but that you yourself also walk orderly, keeping the Law.</u>

The concern is that Paul is teaching and telling others to not do and teach the Law of God just as Christ in Matthew 5:17-19 tells us that we are supposed to do and teach others to follow the Law of God. Suggesting a Nazarite vow would also mean offering a sacrifice. This would show everyone that there was no truth to the rumors that Paul was teaching against obeying God's Law.

Acts 21:26 Then Paul took the men, and the next day, <u>purifying himself along with them</u>, went into the temple giving notice of the completion of the days of purification, <u>until the sacrifice was offered for each one of them.</u>

What did Paul do? He offered the sacrifice. What did the men of Judea who bore false reports do?

Acts 21:30 Then <u>all the city was provoked, and the people rushed together, and taking hold of Paul they dragged him out of the temple</u>, and immediately the doors were shut. 31 <u>While they were seeking to kill him,</u> a report came up to the commander of the Roman cohort that all Jerusalem was in confusion.

They tried to kill him. Let's continue on to Colossians in a more detailed account of these men.

Colossians 2: <u>See to it that no one takes you captive through philosophy and empty deception, according to the tradition of men,</u> according <u>to the elementary principles of the world,</u> rather than according to Christ. 9 For in Him all the fullness of Deity dwells in bodily form, 10 and in Him you have been made complete, and <u>He is the head over all rule and authority;</u> 11 and <u>in Him you were also circumcised with a circumcision made without hands, in the removal of the body of the flesh by the circumcision of Christ;</u> 12 having been buried with Him in baptism, in which you were also raised up with Him through faith in the working of God, who raised Him from the dead. 13 <u>When you were dead in your transgressions and the uncircumcision of your flesh,</u> He made you alive together with Him, <u>having forgiven us all our transgressions, 14 having canceled out the certificate of debt consisting of decrees against us, which was hostile to us; and He has taken it out of the way, having nailed it to the cross.</u> 15 When <u>He had disarmed the rulers and authorities, He made a public display of them, having triumphed over them through Him.</u>

Paul points out that these Judaizers who were trying to stop gentiles from being part of the congregation unless they were circumcised in the flesh, that they were employing a hollow and deceptive philosophy based on men's traditions, not based on the Law of God. He continued to make the point that gentiles *are* circumcised by the higher authority of Christ and therefore are part of Israel regardless of what these men were trying to insist. In Galatians 5, he wishes they'd cut their whole member off so that they might not reproduce. He warns that undergoing manmade traditions for the sake of trying to gain access to

God is a false gospel. If you're trying to approach God by something you do in a transactional sense, then you miss the point entirely and aren't regarding the work of Christ. Instead, you're submitting to a headship and authority of these Pharisaic men.

> Galatians 5:2-12 Behold I, Paul, say to you that if you receive circumcision, Christ will be of no benefit to you. 3 And I testify again to every man who receives circumcision, that he is under obligation to keep the whole Law. 4 You have been severed from Christ, you who are seeking to be justified by law; you have fallen from grace. 6 For in Christ Jesus neither circumcision nor uncircumcision means anything, but faith working through love. 7 You were running well; who hindered you from obeying the truth? 8 This persuasion did not come from Him who calls you. 9 A little leaven leavens the whole lump of dough. 10 I have confidence in you in the Lord that you will adopt no other view; but the one who is disturbing you will bear his judgment, whoever he is. 11 But I, brethren, if I still preach circumcision, why am I still persecuted? Then the stumbling block of the cross has been abolished. 12 I wish that those who are troubling you would even mutilate themselves.

That group of men who were substituting the *gift* of salvation with a false gospel, a gospel that asserts one's salvation was purchased by the blood of one's own foreskin. This group was not in any way, shape, or form preaching the Law of God or the Gospel of Yeshua, but were teaching the traditions of men as if they were the commands of God. Paul continued to encourage gentile converts to not let these Judaizers who are teaching heresies judge them against obedience to God's commands, which are the blueprint of how we are to live like Christ.

Colossians 2 :16-23 Therefore no one is to act as your judge in regard to food or drink or in respect to a festival or a new moon or a Sabbath day— 17 things which are a shadow of what is to come; but the substance belongs to Christ. 18 Let no one keep defrauding you of your prize by delighting in self-abasement and the worship of the angels, taking his stand on visions he has seen, inflated without cause by his fleshly mind 19 and not holding fast to the head, from whom the entire body, being supplied and held together by the joints and ligaments, grows with a growth which is from God.
20 If you have died with Christ to the elementary principles of the world, why, as if you were living in the world, do you submit yourself to decrees, such as, 21 "Do not handle, do not taste, do not touch!" 22 (which all refer to things destined to perish with use)—in accordance with the commandments and teachings of men? 23 These are matters which have, to be sure, the appearance of wisdom in self-made religion and self-abasement and severe treatment of the body, but are of no value against fleshly indulgence.

We aren't keeping the law to be saved, we are saved and obeying God's Law because we now are redeemed from being lawbreakers—redeemed lawbreakers who don't want to return to lawbreaking. Those who preach ritual circumcision are detached from the ways of God and are not holding fast to the head, which is Christ. They are the ones delighting in manmade religion, not the truth of God's word. Paul points out that these men are the ones that hold to the doctrines of "do not handle, do not taste, do not touch". We have examples of Christ himself rebuking these men and their doctrine:

Mark 7:1-8 <u>The Pharisees and some of the scribes</u> gathered around Him when they had come from Jerusalem, 2 and had seen that some of His disciples were eating their bread with impure hands,<u> that is, unwashed.</u> 3 (For <u>the Pharisees and all the Jews</u> <u>do</u> <u>not</u> <u>eat</u> unless they carefully wash their hands, <u>thus observing the traditions of the elders</u>; 4 and when they come from the market place, they<u> do</u> <u>not</u> <u>eat</u> unless they cleanse themselves; and there are many other things which they have received in order to observe, such as the washing of cups and pitchers and copper pots.) 5 <u>The Pharisees and the scribes</u> *asked Him, "Why do Your disciples not walk ac<u>cording to the tradition of the elders</u>, but eat their bread with impure hands?" 6 And He said to them, "Rightly did Isaiah prophesy of you hypocrites, as it is written: '<u>This people honors Me with their lips, But their heart is far away from Me.</u> 7 'But in vain do they worship Me, <u>Teaching as doctrines the precepts of men.</u>'8 <u>Neglecting the</u> <u>commandment</u> <u>of</u> <u>God</u>, <u>you hold to the tradition of men</u>."9 He was also saying to them, "<u>You are experts at setting aside the commandment of God</u> <u>in</u> <u>order</u> <u>to</u> <u>keep</u> <u>your</u> <u>tradition.</u>

(As a side note on bread, I highlight the Pharisees' issue of eating with unwashed hands because it seems to completely dismiss the decree of God that one will toil in the dirt and eat the bread from Genesis 3. Also, Christ is the Bread of Life, which we come to when we are dirty and He is the only one who can make us clean.)

Who is Christ rebuking? The Pharisees and some of their scribes. Why? For *not* following the commands of God and instead teaching their own manmade religious customs. What were they saying? That they, not

God, have the authority to determine what is clean and unclean. Ironically enough, indifference to God's Law and what a man eats is Nicolaitan Doctrine, which is also spoken against by Christ. Christ is rebuking them for the heart that rejects the commands of God, not accidentally eating germs. Touching bread that God has already defined as food with unwashed hands doesn't make it not food, nor does it make you unclean because it passes through your system and out.

What *does* defile a person is ignoring God's commands in your heart, where in the New Covenant those commands are written by the Spirit. So, what do they do now with this group of believing Jews who are not part of the Pharisaic Rabbinical authority, who are now having gentiles come in and are not following matters of personal convictions as it pertains to things like fasting? What do they do with gentiles who aren't washing their hands before they eat and are intermingling with those who hold to that custom? How do you keep the peace with those who are of rabbinic persuasion, judging those gentiles and by an extension, maybe judging Christ? Let's look at Romans 14.

> Romans 14:1-4 <u>Now accept the one who is weak in faith,</u> <u>but not for the purpose of passing judgment on his opinions.</u> 2 One person has faith that he may eat all things, but he who is weak eats <u>vegetables only.</u> 3 <u>The one who eats is not to regard with contempt the one who does not eat,</u> and <u>the one who does not eat is not to judge the one who eats, for God has accepted him.</u> 4 Who are you to judge the servant of another? To his own master he stands or falls; and he will stand, for the Lord is able to make him stand.

Opinions. This verse is talking about people's opinions, not imposing laws on others. It's not about God's commandments. Not on the matter of God's law but in regard to eating and not eating, or eating versus only eating vegetables. This is not reducing God's commands to a matter of subjective interpretations; the matter is opinions regarding food, not Divine edicts from God Himself.

> Romans 14:5-12 <u>One person regards one day above another, another regards every day alike. Each person must be fully convinced in his own mind.</u> 6 <u>He who observes the day,</u> observes it for the Lord, <u>and he who eats,</u> does so for the Lord, for he gives thanks to God; and <u>he who eats not,</u> for the Lord he does not eat, and gives thanks to God. 7 For not one of us lives for himself, and not one dies for himself; 8 for if we live, we live for the Lord, or if we die, we die for the Lord; therefore whether we live or die, we are the Lord's. 9 For to this end Christ died and lived again, that He might be Lord both of the dead and of the living. 10 But you, why do you judge your brother? Or you again, why do you regard your brother with contempt? For we will all stand before the judgment seat of God. 11 For it is written,
> "As I live, says the Lord, every knee shall bow to Me,
> And every tongue shall give praise to God."
> 12 So then each one of us will give an account of himself to God.

The matter of opinions is not regarding the keeping of the Sabbath, it's regarding the days in which people were fasting.

Mark 2:18-20 <u>John's disciples and the Pharisees were fasting</u>; and they *came and *said to Him<u>, "Why do John's disciples and the disciples of the Pharisees fast</u>, but Your disciples <u>do not fast?"</u> 19 And Jesus said to them, "While the bridegroom is with them, the attendants of the bridegroom cannot fast, can they? So long as they have the bridegroom with them, they cannot fast. 20 But the days will come when the bridegroom is taken away from them, <u>and then they will fast in that day</u>.

The Pharisees and John's disciples are clearly not one and the same. The matter before them is eating and not eating. Eating unto the Lord and not eating unto the Lord.

Romans 14 :13-23 Therefore let us not judge one another anymore, but rather determine this—not to put an obstacle or a stumbling block in a brother's way. 14 I know and am convinced in the Lord Jesus that nothing is unclean in itself; but to him who thinks anything to be unclean, to him it is unclean. 15 <u>For if because of food</u> your brother is hurt, you are no longer walking according to love. <u>Do not destroy with your food him for whom Christ died.</u> 16 Therefore <u>do not let what is for you a good thing be spoken of as evil</u>; 17 for the kingdom of God is not eating and drinking, but righteousness and peace and joy in the Holy Spirit. 18 <u>For he who in this way serves Christ is acceptable to God and approved by men.</u> 19 So then we pursue the things which make for peace and the building up of one another. 20 Do not tear down the work of God for the sake of food. All things indeed are clean, but they are evil for the man who eats and gives offense. 21 It is good not to eat meat or to drink wine, or to do anything by which your brother stumbles. 22 The faith which you have, have as your own conviction before God. Happy is he who does not condemn himself in what he approves. 23 But he who doubts is condemned if he eats, because his eating is not from faith; and whatever is not from faith is sin.

This passage has nothing to do with the redefinition of unclean animals that provoke God when eaten now being permissible. It has to do with handwashing and fasting on the days that certain groups were fasting. Outside of national days of fasting, such as for Yom Kippur and Purim, fasting is supposed to be a private matter, but these Pharisees were making big shows of it and getting involved in everyone's business:

Matthew 6:16-18 "Whenever you fast, <u>do not put on a gloomy face as the hypocrites do,</u> for <u>they neglect their appearance so that they will be noticed by men when they are fasting.</u> Truly I say to you, they have their reward in full. 17 <u>But you, when you fast, anoint your head and wash your face 18 so that your fasting will not be noticed by men</u>, but by your Father who is in secret; and your Father who sees what is done in secret will reward you.

Romans 14, Colossians 2, Acts 10, Acts 15, and a whole bucket of Scriptures are taken out of their context to make it seem that those obedient to God and God's commands are the Judaizers. The ones who obey the Law of God *because* they are saved are doing it out of love for God and love for their neighbor. They're *not* the ones who are spoken of in 2 Thessalonians:

2 Thessalonians 2:1-12 Now we request you, brethren, with regard to the coming of our Lord Jesus Christ and our gathering together to Him, 2 <u>that you not be quickly shaken from your composure or be disturbed either by a spirit or a message or a letter as if from us,</u> to the effect that the day of the Lord has come. 3 <u>Let no one in any way deceive you</u>, for it will not come unless the apostasy comes first, <u>and the man of lawlessness is revealed</u>, the son of destruction, 4 <u>who opposes and exalts himself above every so-called god or object of worship, so that he takes his seat in the temple of God, displaying himself as being God</u>. 5 Do you not remember that while I was still with you, I was telling you these things? 6 And you know what restrains him now, so that in his time he will be revealed. 7 <u>For the mystery of lawlessness is already at work;</u> only he who now restrains will do so until he is taken out of the way. 8 <u>Then that lawless one will be revealed whom the Lord will slay with the breath of His mouth and bring to an end by the appearance of His coming;</u> 9 that is, <u>the one whose coming is in accord with the activity of Satan</u>, with all power and signs and false wonders, 10 and <u>with all the deception of wickedness for those who perish, because they did not receive the love of the truth so as to be saved. 11 For this reason God will send upon them a deluding influence so that they will believe what is false, 12 in order that they all may be judged who did not believe the truth, but took pleasure in wickedness.</u>

Jude, as the previous chapter illustrated, speaks of these men:

Jude 1:3-4 Beloved, while I was making every effort to write you about our common salvation, I felt the necessity to write to you <u>appealing that you contend earnestly for the faith which</u> <u>was once for all handed down to the saints.</u> 4 For <u>certain</u> <u>persons have crept in unnoticed, those who were long</u> <u>beforehand marked out for this condemnation, ungodly</u> <u>persons who turn the grace of our God into licentiousness and</u> <u>deny our only Master and Lord, Jesus Christ.</u>

The emphasis of Salvation by works is the same coin as emphasis that God's Law is only for the Jews and obeying is bondage for gentiles. They're both going to the right or to the left rather than the straight and narrow path. Salvation has always been a gift given by faith through grace. Gentiles have always been allowed to come to God and join Israel. It was the teachings and the traditions of men that said that they couldn't, and it is the teachings and traditions of men that tell us not to obey God's Law.

Men can, and will, and do say all sorts of things in their struggle for power and dominance. They'll often form committees and governments for that very purpose, but just like Peter said in Acts 5:29, "Then Peter and the other apostles answered and said, We ought to obey God rather than men."

CHAPTER EIGHT

God's Time, Peter, and Church Authority

2 Kings 17:33 They feared the Lord <u>and served their own gods according to the custom of the nations</u> from among whom they had been carried away into exile.

We've discussed God's established dominion. We've discussed the headship and authority of man walking in the dominion of God as a shepherd-priest-cultivator. We've discussed the dynamics of man in his walk—with God or against it—as the potential for acting as spiritual, humble sons of God or as men of flesh in selfish dominance and violence. We've discussed the bride and how the bride is the picture of how the church is supposed to be for the Bridegroom (Yeshua). We've even discussed those in the 1st century church who epitomized the contrast between God's dominion and man's traditions and structure which were set up alongside God's commands. So, having walked through these concepts, let us now turn to the church today.

When you see the pre-existence of the Torah, and you see that God has an unchanging character that has existed forever, you inevitably have to ask yourself the question: how has the church today become so different from the church of the Scriptures? Where was the departure from God's order? Looking at the forth commandment alone, why do so many churches today hold to nine of the commandments but discard the forth? Isn't it the custom of Christ to keep the Sabbath? Didn't Paul and all the disciples also keep the forth commandment?

Matthew 12:8 For the Son of Man **is Lord of the Sabbath**.

If you're like me and believe in Christ's divinity, and that He created the heavens and the earth and then rested, then He is the one who instituted the Sabbath. If He is the institutor of the Sabbath, and if He does not change, why would He rescind it?

> Luke 4:16 And He came to Nazareth, where He had been brought up; and as was His custom, He entered the synagogue **on the Sabbath, and stood up to read**

We can see that He kept the Sabbath, as was His custom.

> Matthew 24:20-21 But **pray** that your flight will not be in the winter, or **on a Sabbath.** 21 For then there will be a great tribulation, such as has not occurred since the beginning of the world until now, nor ever will

He's stating that during the coming tribulation that is going to transpire after His death and resurrection, we should pray that it isn't on a Sabbath because He clearly shows that the Sabbath is to be kept.

> Luke 23:52-56 this man went to Pilate and asked for the body of Jesus. 53 And he took it down and wrapped it in a linen cloth, and laid Him in a tomb cut into the rock, where no one had ever lain. 54 It was the preparation day, and the Sabbath

was about to begin. 55 Now the women who had come with Him out of Galilee followed, and saw the tomb and how His body was laid. 56 Then they returned and prepared spices and perfumes. And on the Sabbath they rested according to the commandment.

The women were still keeping the Sabbath, according to the commands of God.

Acts 13:42 -44 As Paul and Barnabas were going out, the people kept begging that these **things might be spoken to them the next Sabbath**. 43 Now when the meeting of the synagogue had broken up, many of the Jews and of the God-fearing proselytes followed Paul and Barnabas, who, speaking to them, were urging them to continue in the grace of God. 44 **The next Sabbath** nearly the whole city assembled to hear the word of the Lord.

It seems like Paul and the Jews and Greeks were still keeping the Sabbath after the cross.

Acts 18:4 And he was reasoning in the synagogue **every Sabbath** and trying to persuade Jews and Greeks.

Hebrews 4 talks about that same Sabbath:

Hebrews 4:4-11 For He has said somewhere concerning the seventh day: "And God rested on the seventh day from all His works"; 5 and again in this passage, "They shall not enter My rest." 6 Therefore, since it remains for some to enter it, and those who formerly had good news preached to <u>them failed to enter because of disobedience,</u> 7 <u>He again fixes a certain day,</u> "Today," saying through David after so long a time just as has been said before, "Today if you hear His voice, <u>Do not harden your hearts.</u>" 8 For if Joshua had given them rest, He would not have spoken of another day after that. 9 <u>So there remains a Sabbath rest for the people of God.</u> 10 For the one who has entered His rest has himself also rested from his works, <u>as God did from His.</u> 11 <u>Therefore let us be diligent to enter that rest,</u> so that <u>no one will fall, through following the same example of disobedience</u>

Hebrews 4 shows that concerning the seventh day when God rested, those who were disobedient refused to rest on the seventh day as God commanded. Hebrews 3 and 4 both make the comparison to those who came out of Egypt in the wilderness, where God instructed them to obey His commands, but they rebelled against His ways.

Hebrews 3 :7-11 Therefore, just as the Holy Spirit says,
"<u>Today if you hear His voice,</u>
8 <u>Do not harden your hearts as when they provoked Me,</u>
<u>As in the day of trial in the wilderness,</u>
9 Where your fathers <u>tried Me by testing Me,</u>
And saw My works for forty years.
10 "Therefore I was angry with this generation,
And said, '<u>They always go astray in their heart,</u>
<u>And they did not know My ways</u>';
11 As I swore in My wrath,
'They shall not enter My rest.'"

Israel in the wilderness was constantly rejecting God's headship and dominion. They were continually defiant to the King, His rules, His commandments, and His precepts.

Exodus 16:22-30 Now on the sixth day they gathered twice as much bread, two omers for each one. When all the leaders of the congregation came and told Moses, 23 then he said to them, "This is what the Lord meant: Tomorrow is a sabbath observance, a holy sabbath to the Lord. Bake what you will bake and boil what you will boil, and all that is left over put aside to be kept until morning." 24 So they put it aside until morning, as Moses had ordered, and it did not become foul nor was there any worm in it. 25 Moses said, "Eat it today, for today is a sabbath to the Lord; today you will not find it in the field. 26 Six days you shall gather it, but on the seventh day, the sabbath, there will be none."

27 **It came about on the seventh day that some of the people went out to gather, but they found none.** 28 Then the Lord said to Moses, "How long do you refuse to keep My commandments and My instructions? 29 See, **the Lord has given you the sabbath**; therefore He gives you bread for two days on the sixth day. Remain every man in his place; let no man go out of his place on the seventh day." 30 So the people rested on the seventh day.

The Lord has given the Sabbath. In Genesis, it says that God rested on the seventh day. It's His sabbath.

Leviticus 23:1-4 The Lord spoke again to Moses, saying, 2 "Speak to the sons of Israel and say to them, '**The Lord's appointed times** which you shall proclaim as holy convocations—**My appointed times are these:** 3 'For six days work may be done, but on the seventh day there is a sabbath of complete rest, a holy convocation. You shall not do any work; it is a sabbath to the Lord in all your dwellings. 4 '**These are the appointed times of the Lord, holy convocations** which you shall proclaim at the times appointed for them.

It's clear that they're not the Jewish feasts or the Jewish Sabbaths; they're God's appointed times. The Sabbath was established when there was only Him and two people on the earth, long before there was ever a tribe of Judah or a Jew to have claimed the day for themselves.

Matthew 28:1 <u>Now after the Sabbath,</u> as it began to dawn toward the first day of the week, Mary Magdalene and the other Mary came to look at the grave.

Remember, they rested on the Sabbath, as per the commandment. If the Sabbath is still Saturday, the seventh day, then the day after was the resurrection on Sunday, the first day. So what changed? Where did modern protestants deviate from keeping God's sabbath and why?

The church of Rome (Catholics) made the following declarations in the city of Laodicea: Council of Laodicea in **363 A.D** (Emphasis mine):

Canon 29: Christians <u>must not judaize by resting on the</u> <u>Sabbath</u>, but must work on that day,<u> rather </u>honoring<u> the</u> <u>Lord's Day</u> [Sunday]; and, if they can, resting then as Christians. But if any shall be found judaizers, let them be anathema (detestable) from Christ.

Canon 37-39:<u> It is not lawful</u> to receive portions sent from<u> the</u> <u>feasts of Jews</u> or heretics, nor to <u>feast together with them</u>. (God's Holy Days)

<u>It is not lawful</u> to receive <u>unleavened bread from the Jews</u>, nor to be partakers of their impiety. <u>Thou shalt not keep feasts</u> <u>with Hebrews </u>or heretics, nor<u> receive festival offerings from</u> <u>them</u>. Light hath no communion with darkness. Therefore no Christian should <u>celebrate a feast</u> with heretics or Jews,<u> neither</u> <u>should he receive anything connected with these feasts such</u> <u>unleavened bread</u> and the like."

Men sought to change the Law and the appointed times of God. Men decreed like the Pharisees that they were the gatekeepers of the word of God and chose to reject God's Sabbath and His commandments and instead institute their own. It's not the actions of those who are walking in God's dominion to take His instituted holy days and insist that they be altered or kept on different days, or even to not be kept at all.

Daniel 7: 25 <u>He will speak out against the Most High</u> and wear down the saints of the Highest One, and<u> he will intend to</u> <u>make alterations in times </u>and<u> in law</u>; and they will be given into his hand for a time, times, and half a time.

Daniel is a tricky book of prophecy, but one thing is crystal clear is that those who alter the Law and appointed times that God has set are doing so against the Most High and His dominion. We see it warned against in Paul's second letter to the Thessalonians:

2 Thessalonians 2:1-12 Now we request you, brethren, with regard to the coming of our Lord Jesus Christ and our gathering together to Him, 2 that you not be quickly shaken from your composure or be disturbed either by a spirit or a message or a letter as if from us, to the effect that the day of the Lord has come. 3 Let no one in any way deceive you, for it will not come unless the apostasy comes first, and the man of lawlessness is revealed, the son of destruction, 4 who opposes and exalts himself above every so-called god or object of worship, so that he takes his seat in the temple of God, displaying himself as being God. 5 Do you not remember that while I was still with you, I was telling you these things? 6 And you know what restrains him now, so that in his time he will be revealed. 7 For the mystery of lawlessness is already at work; only he who now restrains will do so until he is taken out of the way. 8 Then that lawless one will be revealed whom **the Lord will slay** with the breath of His mouth and bring to an end by the appearance of His coming; 9 that is, the one whose coming is in accord with the activity of Satan, with all power and signs and false wonders, 10 and with all the deception of wickedness for those who perish, because **they did not receive the love of the truth** so as to be saved. 11 **For this reason God will send upon them a deluding influence so that they will believe what is false**, 12 in order that they all may be judged who did not believe the truth, but took pleasure in wickedness.

Yikes. These are the kind of people who Peter warns us about in 2 Peter 3:14-18. They took pleasure in wickedness. What is wickedness again, just to be sure?

Outline of Biblical Usage [?]

/. one who breaks through the restraint of law and gratifies his lusts

Strong's Definitions [?]   (Strong's Definitions Legend)

ἄθεσμος áthesmos, ath'-es-mos; from G1 (as a negative particle) and a derivative of G5087 (in the sense of enacting); lawless, i.e. (by implication) criminal:—wicked.

There are other days of which the departure from God's holy appointed times have taken place, and we have records of men in the early church trying to hold to what is true in God's ways. We have record of Polycrates who claimed to be holding to John the Apostles' teachings, cited by Eusebius. Again, emphasis mine:

> The writer Eusebius recorded that Polycrates of Ephesus, around 195 A.D. wrote the following to **the Roman Bishop Victor who**, as the previous writing showed, wanted all who professed Christ to change Passover **from** the 14th of Nisan **to Sunday**:

> "We observe the exact day; neither adding, nor taking away. For in Asia also great lights have fallen asleep, which shall rise again on the day of the Lord's coming, when he shall come with glory from heaven, and shall seek out all the saints. Among these are Philip, one of the twelve apostles, who fell

asleep in Hierapolis; and his two aged virgin daughters, and another daughter, who lived in the Holy Spirit and now rests at Ephesus; and, moreover, <u>John, who was both a witness and a teacher, who reclined upon the bosom of the Lord</u>, and, being a priest, wore the sacerdotal plate. He fell asleep at Ephesus. And Polycarp in Smyrna, who was a bishop and martyr; and Thraseas, bishop and martyr from Eumenia, who fell asleep in Smyrna. Why need I mention the bishop and martyr Sagaris who fell asleep in Laodicea, or the blessed Papirius, or Melito, the Eunuch who lived altogether in the Holy Spirit, and who lies in Sardis, awaiting the episcopate from heaven, when he shall rise from the dead? <u>All these **observed the fourteenth day of the passover** according to the Gospel, **deviating in no respect,** but following the rule of faith</u>. And I also, Polycrates, the least of you all, do according to the tradition of my relatives, some of whom I have closely followed. For seven of my relatives were bishops; and I am the eighth. <u>And my relatives always observed the day when **the people put away the leaven.**</u> I, therefore, brethren, who have lived sixty-five years in the Lord, and have met with the brethren throughout the world, and have gone through every Holy Scripture, am not affrighted by terrifying words. For those greater than I have said '**We ought to obey God rather than man**'" –

Eusebius. Church History, Book V, Chapter 24. Translated by Arthur Cushman McGiffert. Excerpted from Nicene and Post-Nicene Fathers, Series Two, Volume 1. Edited by Philip Schaff and Henry Wace. American Edition, 1890. Online Edition Copyright © 2004 by K. Knight.

195 A.D. is over 120 years after Christ and they are still keeping the Passover according to the Scriptures. They were still contending with

the Roman church over obedience to the ways of God vs. the doctrines and traditions of men. We know that Paul addressed the church in Corinth, a gentile city, and advised them on how to keep the Passover:

> 1 Corinthians 5:7-8 Clean out the old leaven so that you may be a new lump, just as you are in fact unleavened. For **Christ our Passover also has been sacrificed.** 8 Therefore let us celebrate the feast, not with old leaven, nor with the leaven of malice and wickedness, but with the unleavened bread of sincerity and truth.

Paul is advising the church to keep the Passover, but the Roman Catholic church was seeking to change the Passover from what God has commanded on Saturday to Sunday. Over time, the customs of other pagan nations were incorporated, and the Biblical Passover of God was left behind. The appointed time when we clear out the leaven and remember that Christ is our Passover Lamb who was slain for the world was replaced with fertility symbols that represent spring and new life such as the bunny and the egg. The same is also true for Christmas.

Christmas

Bible Book List ∨

BIBLE (0)   TOPICAL (0)

Did you mean *christian* (7 results)?

Sorry, we didn't find any results for your search. Please try the following:

I know that Christmas is very sentimental for a lot of people, and although the nativity story is true, Christmas isn't. It's a substitution of the actual Biblical holy days that God made, which are entirely centered on Christ. Many of the most beloved Christmas traditions and practices were stolen from pagan festivals and rituals.

On 15 May, 719, Wynfrith (his name at birth) was sent to Germany by Pope Gregory II and given the name Boniface. His mission was to convert the unbelievers in that part of Europe to Christianity. He worked tirelessly in the country destroying idols and pagan temples across Germany and building churches in their place. In 732 he was made an Archbishop and founded or restored the diocese of Bavaria. It was on this trip, around the time of Winter Solstice, that he was said to have come across a group of pagans worshipping an old oak tree. Horrified by what he saw as blasphemy, the all-action Boniface grabbed the nearest axe and hacked down the tree. As he did this he called the pagans to see the power of his God over theirs. The feelings of the locals were understandably mixed, but Boniface's actions seem mainly to have been taken in good spirit, with some of the tales saying he converted the pagans on the spot. This is where the story divides. Some say that Boniface planted a fir tree there, but the most common idea is that a fir tree grew spontaneously in the oak's place. The fir was seen as an image of God and many believed its evergreen character symbolised the everlasting love of the Creator. According to the story, the next year all the pagans in the area had been converted to Christianity and hung decorations from the tree to celebrate what they now called Christmas rather than Winter Solstice. The story spread and soon Christmas trees became the norm in the newly converted Bavaria, and then spread out to become the tinsel strewn, electric lit, bauble hung festival we know today. –Roger Steer, Historian *Boniface and the story of the Christmas tree*

According to historian Roger Steer, St. Boniface struck down the tree that the pagans were worshiping in their pagan customs, and then it was replaced with another tree with the same customs, only now those customs were being used to worship Christ.

> Jeremiah 10:2-5 Thus says the Lord, "Do not learn the way of the nations, And do not be terrified by the signs of the heavens Although the nations are terrified by them; 3 For the customs of the peoples are delusion; Because it is wood cut from the forest, The work of the hands of a craftsman with a cutting tool. 4 "They decorate it with silver and with gold; They fasten it with nails and with hammers So that it will not totter. 5 "Like a scarecrow in a cucumber field are they, And they cannot speak; They must be carried,
> Because they cannot walk! Do not fear them, For they can do no harm, Nor can they do any good."

While this Jeremiah 10 passage doesn't say that these are Christmas trees, it does discuss that the process of cutting down a tree, dragging it indoors and decorating it *is* a pagan custom. This is in agreement with the following sources, emphasis mine.

The Zondervan Pictorial Encyclopedia of the Bible:
> Gradually a number of prevailing practices of the nations into which Christianity came were assimilated and ...were

combined with the religious ceremonies surrounding Christmas. <u>The assimilation of such practices generally represented efforts by Christians to transform or absorb otherwise pagan practices. The Feast of Saturnalia in early Rome, for example,</u> was celebrated for 7 days from the 17th to <u>the 24th of December and was marked by a spirit of merriment, gift giving to children and other forms of entertainment.</u> Gradually, early Christians replaced the pagan feast with the celebration of Christmas; **but many of the traditions of this observance were assimilated and remain to this day a part of the observance of Christmas**. Other nations, the Scandinavians, Germans, French, English and others, have left their mark . . . as well (pp. 804, 805).

The Christian Encyclopedia

<u>Various symbolic elements of the pagan celebration, such as the lighting of candles, evergreen decorations, and the giving of gifts, were adapted</u> to Christian signification. Later as Christianity spread into northern Europ<u>e, the Celtic, Teutonic, and Slavic winter festivals contributed holly, mistletoe, the Christmas tree, bonfires, and similar items.</u>

Unger's Bible Dictionary:

The giving of presents was <u>a Roman custom; while the yule tree and yule log are remnants of old Teutonic nature worship. Gradually</u> <u>the festival sank into mere revelry</u>...The custom was forbidden by an act of parliament in 1555; And the reformation brought in a refinement in the celebration of Christmas by emphasizing it Christian elements.

Again, yikes. The original Christmas was a Saturnalia festival and the Christmas tree was a pagan idol that they were worshiping.

> Deuteronomy 16:21-22 "You shall not plant for yourself an Asherah of any kind of tree beside the altar of the Lord your God, which you shall make for yourself. 22 **You shall not set up for yourself a sacred pillar which the Lord your God hates.**

Setting up these trees as honorable to God in our homes is something that God tells us that we're not supposed to be doing. If God hates that these trees are used in worship, why would we adopt these customs in our profession of love and worship to Him? There's more. It goes back to even 100 A.D. as Justin Martyr even spoke against the customs that would become Christmas. Emphasis is mine again.

> Many of those who say that they confess Jesus, and are called Christians, eat meats offered to idols, and declare that they are by no means injured in consequence. Confessing themselves to be Christians, and admitting the crucified Jesus to be both Lord and Christ, **yet not teaching His doctrines, but those of the spirits of error.** ...[They are those who] teach to blaspheme the Maker of all things, and Christ, who was foretold by Him as coming, and the God of Abraham, and of Isaac, and of Jacob, with whom we have nothing in common, since we know them to be atheists, impious, unrighteous, and

sinful, and **confessors of Jesus in name only,** instead of worshipers of Him. Yet they style themselves Christians, just as certain among the Gentiles inscribe the name of God upon the works of their own hands, and partake in nefarious and impious rites. Some are called Marcians, and some Valentinians, and some Basilidians, and some Saturnilians, and others by other names; each called after the originator of the individual opinion...the name of the father of the particular doctrine" –Justin Martyr Dialogue with Trypho (Chapters 31-47)

Note that each of them was called after the originator of the individual opinion. The problem with this? Huge. We're warned against this in Scripture. Saturnalians adapted the customs of Christmas, just as the Nicolaitans adapted indifference to the ways a man ate and how he lived.

Acts 6:5 The statement found approval with the whole congregation; and they chose Stephen, a man full of faith and of the Holy Spirit, and Philip, Prochorus, Nicanor, Timon, Parmenas and Nicolas, a proselyte from Antioch

Revelation 2:1-7 'I know your deeds and your toil and perseverance, and that you cannot tolerate evil men, and you put to the test those who call themselves apostles, and they are not, and you found them to be false; 3 and you have perseverance and have endured for My name's sake, and have not grown weary. 4 But I have this against you, that you have left your first love. 5 Therefore remember from where you have fallen, and repent and do the deeds you did at first; or else

I am coming to you and will remove your lampstand out of its place—unless you repent. 6 _Yet this you do have, that you hate the deeds of the Nicolaitans, which I also hate._ 7 He who has an ear, let him hear what the Spirit says to the churches. To him who overcomes, I will grant to eat of the tree of life which is in the Paradise of God.'

Revelation 2:13-16 'I know where you dwell, where Satan's throne is; and you hold fast My name, and did not deny My faith even in the days of Antipas, My witness, My faithful one, who was killed among you, where Satan dwells. 14 _But I have a few things against you, because you have there some who hold the teaching of Balaam, who kept teaching Balak to put a stumbling block before the sons of Israel_, to eat things sacrificed to idols and _to commit acts of immorality. 15 So you also have some who in the same way hold the teaching of the Nicolaitans._ 16 Therefore repent; or else I am coming to you quickly, and I will make war against them with the sword of My mouth.

The deeds of the Nicolaitans appear like the ones of the Saturnalians and the drunken debauchery of Rome.

The letter to the church at Pergamum specifically charged them with having seduced people into eating meat offered to idols and into acts of fornication. The decree of the Jerusalem Council (Acts 15:28, 29) had laid down also two specific conditions upon which Gentiles were to be admitted into Christian fellowship: they were to abstain from things offered to idols and from fornication. These were the very regulations which the Nicolaitans violated. They were a people who used Christian liberty as an occasion for the flesh, against such Paul warned (Gal 5:13). The enticement to such a course of action was the pagan society in which Christians lived where eating meat offered to idols was common. Sex relations outside marriage were completely acceptable in such a society. <u>The Nicolaitans attempted to establish a compromise with the pagan society of the Graeco-Roman world that surrounded them. The people most susceptible to such teaching were, no doubt, the upper classes who stood to lose the most by a separation from the culture to which they had belonged before conversion</u> It may be that the doctrine of the Nicolaitans was dualistic. They prob. reasoned that the human body was evil anyway and only the spirit was good. A Christian, therefore, could do whatever he desired with his body because it had no importance. The spirit, on the other hand, was the recipient of grace<u> which meant that grace and forgiveness were his no matter what he did.</u> **They were those ready to compromise with the world,** They were judged by the author of Revelation to be most dangerou<u>s **because the result of their teaching would have conformed Christianity to the world**</u> rather than have Christianity change the world. – Encyclopedia of the Bible, Biblegateway.com

There is a story of John Calvin in 1537 speaking out against Christmas and its customs, taken from Tom Lambert. As usual, the emphasis is mine.

The war on Christmas was joined in 1537, when, <u>under the influence of John Calvin, Christmas passed without celebration</u>. Unfortunately, Geneva's allies, the Bernese insisted on celebrating Christmas, Circumcision, Annunciation and a few other holidays and demanded the Genevans do the same. <u>Calvin, refusing to give into Bernese demands, was exiled from Geneva and the celebration of Christmas reinstated.</u> When Calvin came back to Geneva in 1541 after a period of exile, <u>he began militating for the abolition of the non-Biblical holidays</u>. In 1545, he achieved limited success in seeing the feasts of the Circumcision and Annunciation suppressed, but the war on Christmas was a tougher fight. Finally, in 1550, Calvin managed to get the Genevan authorities to outlaw Christmas and to mandate that communion would be celebrated only on Sundays, <u>and not on "superstitious" pagan dates like December 25.</u> Indeed, on [December] 25, 1550, the city council sat for business as usual, the courts were in session and businesses were all open under penalty of fine. Calvin, as usual, gave his weekday sermon on a book of the Old Testament and noticed something that upset him: there were more people in church than on a typical weekday. A committed soldier in the war on Christmas, Calvin boomed from the pulpit: "I see more people than usual at sermon today. And why? It's Christmas day. And who told you? <u>It seems so [to be a holy day] to poor beasts. There's the fitting label for all who came to sermon today in honor of the feast... But if you think that Jesus Christ was born today, you are beasts, indeed, rabid beasts."</u> –Supplementa Calviniana, volume 5, sermons on Micah, p. 172, lines 20ff, translated

151

from French by The Ranter. Preaching, Praying and Policing the Reform in Sixteenth-Century Geneva, unpublished Ph.D. dissertation by Thomas A. Lambert, University of Wisconsin-Madison, 1998

We have so many citations about the customs of Christmas and how it was debauchery:

> Consequently the Circumcision fell on the first of January. In the ages of paganism, however, the solemnization of the feast was almost impossible, on account of the orgies connected with the Saturnalian festivities, which were celebrated at the same time. Even in our own day the secular features of the opening of the New Year interfere with the religious observance of the Circumcision, and tend to make a mere holiday of that which should have the sacred character of a Holy Day. St. Augustine points out the difference between the pagan and the Christian manner of celebrating the day: pagan feasting and excesses were to be expiated by Christian fasting and prayer. – The Catholic Encyclopedia (P.L., XXXVIII, 1024 sqq.; Serm. cxcvii, cxcviii)

Even renowned Baptist preacher Charles Spurgeon took issue:

> Certainly we do not believe in the present ecclesiastical arrangement called Christmas: first, because we do not believe in the mass at all, but abhor it, whether it be said or sung in Latin or in English; and, secondly, because we find no Scriptural warrant whatever for observing any day as the

birthday of the Savior; and, consequently, its observance is a superstition, because [it is] not of divine authority.

Many would not consider they had kept Christmas in a proper manner, if they did not verge on gluttony and drunkenness.

If there be any day in the year of which we may be pretty sure that **it was not the day** on which the Saviour was born, it is the twenty-fifth of December. –Charles Spurgeon

We have people today who say such proof on the origins of Christmas just doesn't exist, but it's here.

Originally celebrated on December 17, Saturnalia was extended first to three and eventually to seven days. The date has been connected with the winter sowing season, which in modern Italy varies from October to January. Remarkably like the Greek Kronia, it was the liveliest festival of the year. All work and business were suspended. Slaves were given temporary freedom to say and do what they liked, and certain moral restrictions were eased. The streets were infected with a Mardi Gras madness; a mock king was chosen (Saturnalicius princeps); the seasonal greeting io Saturnalia was heard everywhere. The closing days of the Saturnalia were known as Sigillaria, because of the custom of making, toward the end of the festival, presents of candles, wax models of fruit, and waxen statuettes which were fashioned by the sigillarii or manufacturers of small figures in wax and other media. The cult statue of Saturn himself, traditionally bound at the feet with woolen bands, was untied, presumably to come out and join the fun. The influence of the Saturnalia upon the celebrations of Christmas and the New Year has been direct. The fact that Christmas was celebrated on the birthday of the unconquered sun (dies solis invicti nati) gave the season a solar background, connected with the kalends of January (January 1, the Roman New Year) when houses were decorated with greenery and lights, and presents were given to children and the poor. Concerning the gift candles, the Romans had a story that an old prophecy bade the earliest inhabitants of Latium send heads to Hades and phota to Saturn. The ancient Latins interpreted this to mean human sacrifices, but, according to legend, Hercules advised using lights (phos means "light" or "man" according to accent) and not human heads. – Encyclopedia Britannica, Saturnalia entry

...lasts a week; that over, I am a private person, just a man in the street. Secondly, during my week the serious is barred; no business allowed. Drinking and being drunk, noise and games and dice, appointing of kings and feasting of slaves, singing naked, clapping of tremulous hands, an occasional ducking of corked faces in icy water,--such are the functions over which I preside. But the great things, wealth and gold and such, Zeus distributes as he will. –Works of Lucian Vol. IV: Saturnalia, p.108

Rather than continuing to dump citation after citation of the origins of these counterfeit holidays, of which I could fill many more pages, let's bring it back to the Scriptures:

Deuteronomy 12:29-32 "When the Lord your God cuts off before you the nations which you are going in to dispossess, and you dispossess them and dwell in their land, 30 **beware that you are not ensnared to follow them,** after they are destroyed before you, and that you do not inquire after their gods, saying, 'How do these nations serve their gods, that I also may do likewise?' 31 **You shall not behave thus toward the Lord your God,** for every abominable act which the Lord hates they have done for their gods; for they even burn their sons and daughters in the fire to their gods. 32 "Whatever I command you, you shall be careful to do; you shall not add to nor take away from it.

We are not supposed to worship God in the ways that the pagans worship their false gods.

Exodus 32 So all the people tore off the gold rings which were in their ears and brought them to Aaron. 4 Then he took the gold from their hands, and fashioned it with an engraving tool and made it into a cast metal calf; and they said, "This is your god, Israel, who brought you up from the land of Egypt." 5 Now when Aaron saw this, he built an altar in front of it; and Aaron made a proclamation and said, "Tomorrow shall be a feast **to the Lord**."

When we take a day and say this is good enough for us to worship with, when we abandon all the rest of His holy appointed times, are we not as guilty as the adversary? God told Cain that he was offering the wrong sacrifice and to do it right. God killed the sons of Aaron for offering strange fire to God. Now why are we in churches still doing this? Why are we telling people that this is true and this is Biblical? Isn't that a lie?

> Revelation 21:8 But for the cowardly, and unbelieving, and abominable, and murderers, and sexually immoral persons, and sorcerers, and idolaters, and all liars, their part will be in the lake that burns with fire and brimstone, which is the second death.

If we are not preaching the full truth, then who are we seeking to please? Are we guilty of being like those spoken of in Jeremiah 5?

> Jeremiah 5: 30-31 "An appalling and horrible thing Has happened in the land:
> 31 **The prophets prophesy falsely, And the priests rule on their own authority**;
> And My people love it this way! But what will you do when the end comes?

There is a warning for us in this. Do not harden your heart but instead, enter into His rest.

> Ezekiel 13:8-10 Therefore, thus says the Lord God, "Because you have spoken falsehood and seen a lie, therefore behold, I am against you," declares the Lord God. 9 "So My hand will be against the prophets who see false visions and utter lying divinations. They will have no place in the council of My people, nor will they be written down in the register of the house of Israel, nor will they enter the land of Israel, that you may know that I am

the Lord God. 10 It is definitely because they have misled My people by saying, 'Peace!' when there is no peace.

Revelation 21:22-27 I saw no temple in it, for the Lord God the Almighty and the Lamb are its temple. 23 And the city has no need of the sun or of the moon to shine on it, for the glory of God has illumined it, and its lamp is the Lamb. 24 The nations will walk by its light, and the kings of the earth will bring their glory into it. 25 In the daytime (for there will be no night there) its gates will never be closed; 26 and they will bring the glory and the honor of the nations into it; 27 <u>and nothing unclean, and no one who practices abomination and lying, shall ever come into it, but only those whose names are written in the Lamb's book of life.</u>

Are we supposed to believe that Peter, who was consistently *overly* zealous in strength based on self-determination, was the one who shifted the customs of God as the first "Pope"?

Matthew 16: 16-19 Simon Peter answered, "<u>You are the Messiah, the Son of the living God.</u>" 17 Jesus replied, "Blessed are you, Simon son of Jonah, for this was not revealed to you by flesh and blood, but by my Father in heaven. 18 <u>And I tell you that you are Peter</u>, and on <u>this rock</u> I will build my church, and the gates of Hades will not overcome it. 19 I will give you the keys of the kingdom of heaven; whatever you bind on earth will be bound in heaven, and whatever you loose on earth will be loosed in heaven."

Is Christ tossing Peter the figurative keys to be as Christ on earth? What is being said here:

Outline of Biblical Usage [?]

    I. Peter = "a rock or a stone"

       1. one of the twelve disciples of Jesus

Strong's Definitions [?]   (Strong's Definitions Legend)

Πέτρος **Pétros**, pet'-ros; apparently a primary word; a (piece of) rock (larger than G3037); as a name, Petrus, an apostle:—Peter, rock. Compare G2786.

Is Christ saying that Peter is in the place of Christ? No. Here's why:

Psalm 62:2 He **only** is my rock and my salvation,
My stronghold; I shall not be greatly shaken.

Psalm 18:2 The Lord is my rock and my fortress and my deliverer,
My God, my rock, in whom I take refuge;
My shield and the horn of my salvation, my stronghold.

1 Corinthians 3:11 For no man can lay a foundation other than the one which is laid, **which is Jesus Christ**.

The rock is the foundation on which the church is built upon is the revelation of Christ as the Messiah.

1 Corinthians 10:1-4 For <u>I do not want you to be unaware</u>, brethren, that our fathers were all under the cloud and all passed through the sea; 2 and all were baptized into Moses in the cloud and in the sea; 3 and all ate the same spiritual food; 4 <u>and all drank the same spiritual drink, for they were drinking from a spiritual rock which followed them</u>; and **the rock was Christ**.

Christ tells us heeding Him as the rock, as the foundation, as the head, as the authority, is how the church is built.

Matthew 7:24-25 "Therefore <u>everyone who hears these words of Mine</u> and **acts on them**, may be compared to <u>a wise man who built his house on the rock</u>. 25 And the rain fell, and the floods came, and the winds blew and slammed against that house; and yet it did not fall, <u>for it had been founded on the rock.</u>

Christ is calling Peter back to the original purpose of man. To reflect God. To build *with him* as the foundation for everything, not us. We seek His leadership and direction because He is our Bridegroom and He leads us in the way that is good for us as His bride, as an extension of Himself.

Another reason that we know Christ isn't instituting the Catholic hierarchy is because such a hierarchy already existed with the Pharisees who had seated themselves in the position of Moses over believers. He speaks against the practice of their self-elevation and hypocrisy:

Matthew 23:6-12 Then Jesus spoke to the crowds and to His disciples, 2saying: "The scribes and the Pharisees have seated themselves in the chair of Moses; 3 therefore all that they tell you, do and observe, <u>but do not do according to their deeds; for they say things and do not do them.</u> 4<u>They tie up heavy burdens and lay them on men's shoulders, but they themselves are unwilling to move them with so much as a finger.</u> 5 <u>But they do all their deeds to be noticed by men; for they broaden their phylacteries and lengthen the tassels of their garments.</u> 6 <u>They love the place of honor at banquets and the chief seats in the synagogues, 7 and respectful greetings in the market places, and being called Rabbi by men.</u> 8 **But do not be called Rabbi; for One is your Teacher, and** <u>**you are all brothers.**</u> 9 **Do not call anyone on earth your father**; for **One is your Father, He who is in heaven.** 10 **Do not be called leaders; for One is your Leader**, that is, **Christ.** 11 <u>But the greatest among you shall be your servant.</u> 12 Whoever exalts himself shall be humbled; and whoever humbles himself shall be exalted."

Does that sound like Christ is saying establish popes and priests that you call Father? It doesn't sound like it to me.

Ephesians 2:17-22 And <u>He came and preached peace to you who were far away, and peace to those who were near</u>; 18 for <u>through Him we both have our access in one Spirit to the Father.</u> 19 **So then you are no longer strangers and aliens,** but <u>you are fellow citizens with the saints, and are of God's household,</u> 20 <u>having been built on the foundation of the</u>

apostles and prophets, **Christ Jesus Himself being the corner stone**, 21 in whom the whole building, being fitted together, is growing into a holy temple in the Lord, 22 in whom you also are being built together into a dwelling of God in the Spirit.

Ephesians 2 is telling us that Peter, as an ambassador to the Gentiles, was reminded to grow the church and that the gentiles are no longer gentiles once they have crossed over to the revelation of Christ, they are now part of one body, Christ's. So then, what does binding and loosening represent? I think it's the patience of the church for these gentiles who are turning to God in that they were given introductory commands so they wouldn't be barred from coming back to church and learning the rest of them. God is to be regarded as Holy in His temple. When we read the passage stating that we are being built together into a dwelling of God in the Spirit, then God shows great patience with those who are turning from sin. The council in Acts 15 didn't remove the Law of God for gentiles but established grace for those turning to God. Peter loosened those, but bound others.

Acts 5:1-11 But a man named Ananias, with his wife Sapphira, sold a piece of property, 2 and kept back some of the price for himself, with his wife's full knowledge, and bringing a portion of it, he laid it at the apostles' feet. 3 But Peter said, "Ananias, why has Satan filled your heart to lie to the Holy Spirit and to keep back some of the price of the land? 4 While it remained unsold, did it not remain your own? And after it was sold, was it not under your control? **Why is it that you have conceived this deed in your heart? You have not lied to**

men but to God." 5 And as he heard these words, Ananias fell down and breathed his last; and great fear came over all who heard of it. 6 The young men got up and covered him up, and after carrying him out, they buried him.7 Now there elapsed an interval of about three hours, and his wife came in, not knowing what had happened. 8 And <u>Peter responded to her,</u> <u>"Tell me whether you sold the land for such and such a price?"</u> <u>And she said, "Yes, that was the price."</u> 9 Then Peter said to her, <u>"Why is it that you have agreed together to put the Spirit</u> <u>of the Lord to the test</u>? Behold, the feet of those who have buried your husband are at the door, and they will carry you out as well." 10 <u>And immediately she fell at his feet and</u> <u>breathed her last, and the young men came in and found her</u> <u>dead, and they carried her out and buried her beside her</u> <u>husband.</u> 11 And great fear came over the whole church, and over all who heard of these things.

(Note that there are three separate Ananias's in the book of Acts to avoid any confusion.)

There wasn't anything in the prohibitions in Acts 15 regarding keeping money from land. The issue is lying to the Spirit of God, and that's big, no matter where you're from.

We've established that the church drifted away from God's order, his set days, His dominion, and the headship where He is holy and set apart. We've talked about the deeds of the councils of what would become the Catholic church and how 300 some years after the apostles it began to splinter away from the faith of the New Testament church. We've talked about not calling men Rabbi or Teacher in the hierarchical sense. What is the structure of the church supposed to look like?

> Matthew 20:25-28 But Jesus called them to Himself and said, "You know that the rulers of the Gentiles lord it over them, and their great men exercise authority over them. 26 **It is not this way among you, but whoever wishes to become great among you shall be your servant**, 27 and whoever wishes to be first among you shall be your slave; 28 just as the Son of Man did not come to be served, but to serve, and to give His life a ransom for many."

I've been around a lot of churches in my walk with God. I've been in places that have no engagement with new attendees as if they really do not care to reach the community around them. I've also seen some of the most gracious and humble and loving pastors who reason with people in the Word through much personal sacrifice of their personal time and resources because they have genuine hearts for the purpose of God's people. What about that? What about the position of pastors? The Bible does tell us that that there are overseers, and these are the qualifications of them:

> Titus 1:5-9 For this reason I left you in Crete, that you would set in order what remains and appoint elders in every city as I directed you, 6 namely, if any **man** is **above reproach**, the husband of one wife, having children who believe, not accused of dissipation or rebellion. 7 For the overseer must be **above reproach** as **God's steward**, not self-willed, not quick-tempered, not addicted to wine, not pugnacious, not fond of

sordid gain, 8 but <u>**hospitable, loving what is good, sensible, just, devout, self-controlled**</u>, 9 holding fast the faithful word which is in accordance with the teaching, so that he will be **able both to exhort in sound doctrine and to refute those who contradict.**

Look at most of the churches in America. Most of the men are not qualified. We have mega church pastors with stadium seating and they're churning out books that are speaking of having your best life here in the flesh rather than in the promise with God. So many of these men sell books, music and market things for sordid gain. They do not teach that which is able to exhort in sound doctrine, but rather they promote a relativistic, muddled, and opinionated, world-based "morality" that is not rooted in the Scripture but champions the distortion of it. So many of these men are not able to correct lies and challenges to the faith because they have no true faith, they are as the ones spoken of in Matthew 7:

Matthew 7:15-22 **Beware of the false prophets**, <u>who come to you in sheep's clothing</u>, but <u>inwardly are ravenous wolves.</u> 16 <u>You will know them by their fruits.</u> Grapes are not gathered from thorn bushes nor figs from thistles, are they? 17 So every good tree bears good fruit, but the bad tree bears bad fruit. 18 A good tree cannot produce bad fruit, nor can a bad tree produce good fruit. 19 <u>Every tree that does not bear good fruit is cut down and thrown into the fire.</u> 20 So then, you will know them by their fruits. 21 **Not everyone who says to Me, 'Lord, Lord,' will enter the kingdom of heaven**, but <u>**he who does the will of My Father who is in heaven will**</u>

enter. 22 <u>Many will say to Me on that day, 'Lord, Lord, did we</u> <u>not prophesy in Your name, and in Your name cast out</u> <u>demons, and in Your name perform many miracles?'</u> 23 And then <u>I will declare to them, 'I never knew you;</u> **depart from** **Me, you who practice lawlessness.**

I've approached many pastors about what I have heard them preach in sermons that did not line up with the Word of God. With the majority of pastors I have challenged with something that I saw as contrary to Scripture, they're usually pretty humble about it. Most of them won't (or shouldn't) boot you out the door or call you names, such as divisive or heretic, or say that you're like Korah. However, I've seen both sides of the coin. I've seen pastors humbly submit that they may have been wrong when confronted and repent. I love it when that happens, as these brothers in the faith recognize they are not infallible and they too can make mistakes.

Then there are those times where you may see a pastor get up there slandering and slaying demons, saying that he's going to shake the gates of hell and that the devil is an idiot. You know, all those things that the book of Jude tells us not to do. Sometimes, they might get a little self-righteous and tell you that they're a warrior (even though you see several places in Scripture saying they're supposed to be sheep or shepherds). Sometimes to emphasize what they are saying, they'll declare something like, "I've got a revelation from God," and claim they're "God's anointed," or monologue about how "David killed the men that raised the sword to Saul so *how dare you levy an accusation against them!*" They may or may not start backing up in anticipation of some giant sinkhole ready to open up and swallow you whole.

Here is an excellent definition of discernment: Knowing the difference between right, and almost right. Moses was anointed and exalted as a leader of God. He also was the humblest man on Earth:

> Numbers 12:3 Now the man Moses was very humble, more than any man who was on the face of the earth.

Moses didn't assemble men together that he might be made their leader. God called Moses, Moses argued with God a little bit and God said for him to go. When the sons of Korah said that they were appointed just the same as Moses, Moses didn't behave rashly. He didn't puff out his chest and start throwing insults, rebukes, and slurs. He humbled himself to the ground before God and God again established Moses as the one who was in leadership. God showed His dominion and order against the dominance of men. The Earth opened up and swallowed Korah. They rebelled. The sons of Korah's rebellion were put at the door of the tent of meeting in contrast to their fathers.

Now, if you're bringing something up that you see as a violation of the commands of God, directly from the Savior, and the response is hostility, there is a pretty solid chance that your "overseer" isn't as above reproach as they might like to think they are, especially if they're a little quick tempered in that "warrior" status. When they're telling you that you have no right to "bring an accusation" against them, they are drawing the comparison that they are at best Moses, and at the very least, a priest of God. How dare you challenge the word of a priest of God! That's some scary business to be meddling in.

I mean, I would not want to challenge a legitimate priest of God, performing their temple sacrifices and priestly duties. Isn't that kind of a straw man, though? It can be intimidating for a regular guy who sees a biblical issue to speak to this kind of person who has his own "self" built up in his mind, in order to scare people into not confronting him with things he says or does that might not be in line with Scripture. There is a lot of ego at play here, and it's often not easy to recognize. After all, most of us come from churches where the mindset is that the more knowledge of preach-able, pulpit-worthy stuff one has means that they are way holier than you.

> Acts 4:5-12 On the next day, <u>their rulers and elders and scribes</u> were gathered together in Jerusalem; 6 and <u>Annas</u> **the high priest** was there, and Caiaphas and John and Alexander, **and all who were of high-priestly descent.** 7 When they had placed them in the center, they began to inquire, "<u>By what power, or in what name, have you done this?</u>" 8 Then <u>Peter, filled with the Holy Spirit,</u> said to them, "<u>Rulers and elders of the people,</u> 9 if we are on trial today for a benefit done to a sick man, as to how this man has been made well, 10 <u>let it be known to all of you and to all the people of Israel, that by the name of Jesus Christ the Nazarene, whom you crucified, whom God raised from the dead—by this name this man stands here before you in good health. 11 He is the stone which was rejected by you, the builders, but which became the chief corner stone. 12 And there is salvation in no one else; for there is no other name under heaven that has been given among men by which we must be saved.</u>"

These men were standing in front of the religious scholars, the seminaries, the men who were knowledgeable about reading the Scriptures day in and day out, the educated pastors, the ones who are so self-assured in their ways, these men are asking the questions of John and Peter, fishermen.

> Acts 4:13-21 Now as they observed **the confidence** of Peter and John and **understood that they were uneducated and untrained men,** they were amazed, and **began to recognize them as having been with Jesus**. 14 And seeing the man who had been healed standing with them, they had nothing to say in reply. 15 But when they had ordered them to leave the Council, they began to confer with one another, 16 saying, "What shall we do with these men? For the fact that a noteworthy miracle has taken place through them is apparent to all who live in Jerusalem, and we cannot deny it. 17 But so that it will not spread any further among the people, let us warn them to speak no longer to any man in this name." 18 And when they had summoned them, they commanded them not to speak or teach at all in the name of Jesus. 19 But Peter and John answered and said to them, **"Whether it is right in the sight of God to give heed to you rather than to God, you be the judge; 20 for we cannot stop speaking about what we have seen and heard."** 21 When they had threatened them further, they let them go (finding no basis on which to punish them) on account of the people, because they were all glorifying God for what had happened

Take a moment and carefully evaluate what your church leaders are saying. If they are specifically underscoring certain things without proper context, your church may be in trouble. If your church pastor or overseer is quoting Titus out of context...

Titus 3:10-11 As for a person who stirs up division, after warning him once and then twice, have nothing more to do with him, 11 knowing that such a person is warped and sinful; he is self-condemned.

...to say that someone attempting genuine accountability of leadership in accordance with Scripture is "stirring up division after a warning," that pastor would take it up with the Savior. The Savior is divisive.

John 7:40-43Some of the people therefore, when they heard these words, were saying, "This certainly is the Prophet." 41 Others were saying, "This is the Christ." Still others were saying, "Surely the Christ is not going to come from Galilee, is He? 42 Has not the Scripture said that the Christ comes from the descendants of David, and from Bethlehem, the village where David was?" 43 **So a division occurred in the crowd because of Him**. 44 Some of them wanted to seize Him, but no one laid hands on Him.

Christ is divisive from the world that seeks its own dominion and control. Truth is divisive from error. Holiness is divisive from wickedness. To label all accountability as division and all division as wickedness is to slander Christ. Speaking of slandering Christ...

CHAPTER NINE

Satan and the Sovereignty of God

Can you have a book about God's divine authority and dominion and headship without mentioning the most notorious rebellion in recorded history? Satan, once known as Lucifer. I could skip this topic because I don't really like spending much time or focusing on him. I debated with myself on having the entirety of this chapter simply read, "Don't focus on Satan, Focus on God" and then move on to chapter 10, but I think that there are a few points that do need to be made because, as it were, there are issues surrounding the adversary. Questions like, "How does Satan fit in the context of God's Sovereignty. Is Satan the king of Salem? What was all that about? I'll try to make this chapter short but cut to the quick of the matter.

Have you ever encountered those who are convinced that there is a demon under every leaf? Have you ever been to a church like I mentioned in previous chapters that when members encounter any opposition, they begin to slander and revile the adversary? Why? Why is there so much focus and emphasis on the devil? Is it because of the armor of God?

> Ephesians 6:11-17 Put on the full armor of God, <u>so that you will be able to stand firm against the schemes of the devil. 12 For our struggle is not against flesh and blood, but against the</u>

rulers, against the powers, against the world forces of this darkness, against the spiritual forces of wickedness in the heavenly places. 13 Therefore, take up the full armor of God, so that you will be able to resist in the evil day, and having done everything, to stand firm. 14 Stand firm therefore, having girded your loins with truth, and having put on the breastplate of righteousness, 15 and having shod your feet with the preparation of the gospel of peace; 16 in addition to all, taking up the shield of faith with which you will be able to extinguish all the flaming arrows of the evil one. 17 And take the helmet of salvation, and the sword of the Spirit, which is the word of God.

Does that passage say "gear up and smack the devil in the face and burst through the gates of hell and start drop kicking evil"?

Jude 1:8-11 Yet in the same way these men, also by dreaming, defile the flesh, and reject authority, and revile angelic majesties. 9 But Michael the archangel, when he disputed with the devil and argued about the body of Moses, did not dare pronounce against him a railing judgment, but said, "The Lord rebuke you!" 10 But these men revile the things which they do not understand; and the things which they know by instinct, like unreasoning animals, by these things they are destroyed. 11 Woe to them! For they have gone the way of Cain, and for pay they have rushed headlong into the error of Balaam, and perished in the rebellion of Korah.

Can that be right? How can we reconcile these passages?

Ephesians 6:10 Finally, <u>be strong in the Lord </u>and <u>in the strength of **His** might</u>.

That's where the important context of that entire armor of God passage starts. The armor of God is an endurance measure as we submit to *His* might and *His* strength. We resist temptation by focusing on Him and submitting to His will. Getting emotional in a hyped-up, angry rage is not a fruit of the Spirit.

James 1:19-20 This you know, my beloved brethren. But everyone must be quick to hear, <u>slow to speak and slow to anger</u>; 20for <u>the anger of man does not achieve the righteousness of God</u>.

Think of Job who we mentioned in previous chapters. Satan had to get permission from God to afflict Job. God had to allow Job's affliction.

Job 2:3-6 <u>The Lord said to Satan, "Have you considered My servant Job?</u> For there is no one like him on the earth, a blameless and upright man fearing God and turning away from evil<u>. And he still holds fast his integrity, although you incited Me against him to ruin him without cause."</u> 4 Satan answered the Lord and said, "Skin for skin! Yes, all that a man has he will give for his life. 5 However, put forth Your hand now, and touch his bone and his flesh; he will curse You to Your face." 6 <u>So the Lord said to Satan, "Behold, he is in your power, only spare his life."</u>

God, in His divine purpose, gave Satan permission to afflict Job, and even then, He set perimeters as to what Satan was allowed to do. Satan didn't have the jurisdiction to do anything without God having given it to him.

2 Thessalonians 2:7-12 For the mystery of lawlessness is already at work; <u>only he who now restrains will do so until he is taken out of the way</u>. 8 Then that lawless one will be revealed <u>whom the Lord will slay with the breath of His mouth</u> and bring to an end by the appearance of His coming; 9 that is, the one whose coming is in accord with the activity of Satan, with all power and signs and false wonders, 10 and with all the deception of wickedness for those who perish, because they did not receive the love of the truth so as to be saved. 11 **For this reason God will send upon them a deluding influence so that they will believe what is false**, 12 in order that they all may be judged who did not believe the truth, but took pleasure in wickedness.

God allows people who do not love the truth to be under delusions and afflicted by spirits. We are either in submission to His authority and dominion, walking in His purpose, or we are delusional and seeking our own dominance, walking in submission to delusions that He's sent or allowed.

Lamentations 3:37- 38 <u>Who is there who speaks and it comes to pass</u>, **Unless the Lord has commanded it?** 38 <u>Is it not from **the mouth of the Most High**</u> That <u>both good and ill go forth?</u>

Look at these passages from 1 Samuel:

> 1 Samuel 16: 14 Now <u>the Spirit of the Lord departed from Saul</u>, and <u>an evil spirit from the Lord</u> terrorized him.
> 1 Samuel 18: 10 Now it came about on <u>the next day that an evil spirit from God came mightily upon Saul</u>, and he raved in the midst of the house, while David was playing the harp with his hand, as usual; and a spear was in Saul's hand.
>
> 1 Samuel 19: <u>9 Now there was an evil spirit from the Lord on Saul as he was sitting in his house with his spear in his hand,</u> and David was playing the harp with his hand.

Why did God send evil to Saul? Why does God send evil at all?

> Romans 1:18-24 <u>For the wrath of God is revealed from heaven against all ungodliness and unrighteousness of men who suppress the truth in unrighteousness,</u> 19 because that which is known about God is evident within them; for God made it evident to them. 20 For since the creation of the world His invisible attributes, His eternal power and divine nature, have been clearly seen, being understood through what has been made, so that they are without excuse. <u>21 For even though they knew God, they did not honor Him as God or give thanks, but they became futile in their speculations, and their foolish heart was darkened. 22 Professing to be wise, they became fools,</u> 23 and <u>exchanged the glory of the incorruptible God for an image in the form of corruptible man</u> and of birds and four-footed animals and crawling creatures.24 <u>Therefore God gave them</u>

175

over in the lusts of their hearts to impurity, so that their bodies would be dishonored among them.

Saul exchanged the glory of God for a corruptible man.

> 1 Samuel 15:12 Samuel rose early in the morning to meet Saul; and it was told Samuel, saying, "Saul came to Carmel, and behold, he set up a monument for himself, then turned and proceeded on down to Gilgal."

Saul, like so many who slander and revile the servants of God, built himself up by giving glory to himself in Christ, rather than giving glory to God where it belongs.

> Isaiah 42:8 "I am the Lord, that is My name; I will not give My glory to another, Nor My praise to graven images.

Think again about those who charge the gates of hell in their fiery speeches:

> Luke 22:31 "Simon, Simon, behold, Satan has demanded **permission** to sift you like wheat

Satan wanted permission. He didn't take control because he couldn't; the control was in the hands of God. If you're being attacked and afflicted by the adversary, it is with God's allowance. It's with God's permission. Why? For either your humbling or His glory, but either way, you need to focus on Him.

Isaiah 45:5-7 "<u>I am the Lord, and there is no other;</u>
Besides Me there is no God.
<u>I will gird you</u>, though you have not known Me;
6 <u>That men may know from the rising to the setting of the sun</u>
That there is no one besides Me.
<u>I am the Lord, and there is no other,</u>
7 **<u>The One forming light and creating darkness,</u>**
<u>Causing well-being and creating calamity</u>;
I am the Lord who does all these.

The big talk and slander of the spiritual matters is to speak boldly against God's authority. Rather, intercede with God. Direct your questions and complaints to Him alone. God allows people to be tested and tempted by the adversary. When we reject submission to God—His order, His cleanliness—we choose death, disorder, chaos, and uncleanliness. When we choose the ways contrary to God, we embrace the jurisdiction of the adversary. We remove ourselves from the presence and protection of God. The adversary only has the authority to do what God permits or we allow.

CHAPTER TEN

Adultery, Polygamy, and God

We've spoken about God's authority and headship. We've spoken about how man is supposed to be that reflection of God to his bride, and how that bride is to reflect the bride of Christ. In submission to God's will and His rulership and authority, we're walking in that covenant relationship as one who walks with the bridegroom. I'd like to look now at the concepts surrounding our marriage to the Creator of heaven and earth. If marriage is a parallel of God and our marriage to Him, then we'd see such matters of adultery and polygamy as directly oppositional. Whenever polygamy is favorably mentioned in certain faith communities and sects, a few points are usually brought up:

1. David had multiple wives and was a man after God's own heart.
2. The Bible never says polygamy is wrong.
3. Joash had two wives.

As I looked at the Scriptures regarding David, these passages stood out to me:

Deuteronomy 17:17 He shall **not** multiply wives for himself, or else his heart will turn away; nor shall he greatly increase silver and gold for himself.

1 Samuel 25:43 David had also taken Ahinoam of Jezreel, and they both became his wives.

2 Samuel 11:14-15 14 Now in the morning David wrote a letter to Joab and sent it by the hand of Uriah. 15He had written in the letter, saying, "Place Uriah in the front line of the fiercest battle and withdraw from him, so that he may be struck down and die."

1 Chronicles 28:3 "But God said to me, 'You shall not build a house for My name because you are a man of war and have shed blood.'

David was in violation of this prohibition against taking multiple wives. God watched as that sin grew into a greater sin. David did turn his heart from the ways of God when he committed adultery with Bathsheba. He then made it worse when he committed violence against Uriah. Then David rounded it out and took Bathsheba to be his wife. That is three sins, not one. Adultery, murder, and polygamy. Remember what God said in Genesis?

Genesis 2:24 Therefore a man shall leave his father and his mother and hold fast to his wife, and they shall become one flesh.

The one wife. Not wives. This is again affirmed in Matthew 19:

Matthew 19:5 For this reason a man shall leave his father and mother and be joined to his wife, and the two shall become one flesh.

If the parallel of us entering the marriage covenant with God is that we are like the bride and Him the Bridegroom, then polygamy and adultery would be the parallel of us saying we love God, while we cheat on Him with other gods. There seems to be a correlation to either violence or the turning of one's heart away from trusting God that occurs when polygamy is involved. A case can be made from Genesis as mentioned in the chapter about the Nephilim.

Genesis 4: 19 Lamech took to himself two wives: the name of the one was Adah, and the name of the other, Zillah.

Genesis 4: 22 As for Zillah, she also gave birth to Tubal-cain, the forger of all implements of bronze and iron; and the sister of Tubal-cain was Naamah.23 Lamech said to his wives, "Adah and Zillah, Listen to my voice, You wives of Lamech, Give heed to my speech, For I have killed a man for wounding me; And a boy for striking me; 24 If Cain is avenged sevenfold, Then Lamech seventy-sevenfold."

Genesis 6:2 ...that the sons of God saw that the daughters of men were beautiful; and they took wives for themselves, whomever they chose.

Genesis 6:13 Then God said to Noah, "The end of all flesh has come before Me; for the earth is filled with violence because of them; and behold, I am about to destroy them with the earth."

Lamech took two wives and then he killed a man for wounding him and killed a boy for striking him. He likens this killing to Cain, his father, the first murderer. Next thing we see is Lamech's son making instruments of war. Then it says that the sons of God took whatever wives they liked—potentially in addition to the ones that they already had—then the earth was filled with violence and the world is destroyed.

> 1 Kings 11:3 -6 He had seven hundred wives, princesses, and three hundred concubines, and his wives turned his heart away.4 For when Solomon was old, his wives turned his heart away after other gods; and his heart was not wholly devoted to the LORD his God, as the heart of David his father had been. 5For Solomon went after Ashtoreth the goddess of the Sidonians and after Milcom the detestable idol of the Ammonites. 6Solomon did what was evil in the sight of the LORD, and did not follow the LORD fully, as David his father had done.

Solomon, who built the temple of the Lord, took way too many wives. Instead of being the example of Christ as King who has one bride, he had his heart led astray to follow after other gods. There seems to be a Scriptural connection to the fleshly desire and lust for more than one wife and the perversion of purpose and headship that God established at creation. A supporter of polygamy once argued with me that God said He gave David Saul's wives, so that must mean that God supports polygamy. For a second, when I first heard this, I thought "what an interesting objection". Then I read the passage in question and saw that the context was that God is the one who provides everything that David has ever needed all the days of his life. If David needed food, God had provided it. God gave David favor, gave him bread, gave him the entire kingdom of Israel and Judah. If there was some reason that David needed more than one wife, it wasn't for David to determine. God would have determined that and given him more than one wife.

> 2 Samuel 12:7-12 Nathan then said to David, "You are the man! Thus says the Lord God of Israel, 'It is I who anointed you king over Israel and it is I who delivered you from the hand of Saul. 8 I also gave you your master's house and your master's wives **into your care**, and I gave you the house of Israel and Judah; and if that had been too little, I would have added to you many more things like these! 9 <u>Why have you despised the word of the Lord by doing evil in His sight?</u> You have struck down Uriah the Hittite with the sword, <u>have taken his wife to be your wife</u>, and have killed him with the sword of the sons of Ammon. 10 Now therefore, the sword shall never depart from your house, <u>because you have despised Me and have taken the wife of Uriah the Hittite to be your wife.</u>' 11 Thus says the Lord, 'Behold, I will raise up evil against you from your own household; <u>I will even take your wives before your eyes and give them to your companion, and he will lie with your wives in broad daylight.</u> 12 Indeed you did it secretly, but I will do this thing before all Israel, and under the sun.'"

See that in verse 10? God says that David despised Him and took the wife of Uriah. He calls out David for despising the Word of the Lord. This is not an endorsement of polygamy. This is a rebuke. Look at the punishment that followed. God says that because of the evil David did in taking wives, his offspring Absolom will also do so to him, publicly. Another reason we know God wasn't saying "hey, you need more wives,

I'll give you Saul's wives" is because God already stated that this is against His will. David is married to Saul's daughter.

> Deuteronomy 27:23 'Cursed is he who lies with his mother-in-law.' And all the people shall say, 'Amen.'

The fruit of David taking multiple wives is the death of so many people. There are more examples

> Judges 8:27-32 Gideon made it into an ephod, and placed it in his city, Ophrah, and all Israel played the harlot with it there, so that it became a snare to Gideon and his household.
> 28 So Midian was subdued before the sons of Israel, and they did not lift up their heads anymore. And the land was undisturbed for forty years in the days of Gideon.
> 29 Then Jerubbaal the son of Joash went and lived in his own house. 30 Now Gideon had seventy sons who were his direct descendants, for he had many wives. 31 His concubine who was in Shechem also bore him a son, and he named him Abimelech. 32 And Gideon the son of Joash died at a ripe old age and was buried in the tomb of his father Joash, in Ophrah of the Abiezrites.

Gideon, who was a righteous judge of Israel, even wandered into apostasy and played the harlot in adultery against God.

> 2 Chronicles 11:22 Rehoboam appointed Abijah the son of Maacah as head and leader among his brothers, for he intended to make him king. 23 He acted wisely and distributed some of

his sons through all the territories of Judah and Benjamin to all the fortified cities, and he gave them food in abundance. And he sought many wives for them.

2 Chronicles 12: When the kingdom of Rehoboam was established and strong, he and all Israel with him forsook the law of the Lord. 2 And it came about in King Rehoboam's fifth year, because they had been unfaithful to the Lord, that Shishak king of Egypt came up against Jerusalem.

King Rehoboam sought many wives for himself and then he and all of Israel forsook the law of God and were unfaithful. They cheated on God. They failed to represent the husbandly dominion of our King to His bride.

2 Chronicles 24:2 Joash did what was right in the sight of the Lord all the days of Jehoiada the priest. 3 Jehoiada took two wives for him, **and** he became the father of sons and daughters.

2 Chronicles 24: 20 Then the Spirit of God came on Zechariah the son of Jehoiada the priest; and he stood above the people and said to them, "Thus God has said, 'Why do you transgress the commandments of the Lord and do not prosper? Because you have forsaken the Lord, He has also forsaken you.'" 21 So they conspired against him and at the command of the king they stoned him to death in the court of the house of the Lord. 22 Thus Joash the king did not remember the kindness which his father Jehoiada had shown him, but he murdered his son. And as he died he said, "May the Lord see and avenge!"

This one was interesting, because all three sinful elements are here: multiplying wives, then, forsaking God, and then engaging in violence. How do we then reconcile verses two and three since God doesn't seem to endorse taking multiple wives, but it looks like the favor was upon him? To answer that, here is a quote.

> Some take this to mean that Jehoida gave Joash two wives at the same time and since Joash is said to have "done what was right in the sight of the Lord," it must mean that polygamy is right in the sight of God. There are lots of problems with this interpretation. First, there is nothing here that requires us to read this in a polygamous way. For example, Joash could have had one wife, and then she died, and then he was is given another, and Jehoida is the one who arranged a godly wife for the king. That's a possible reading of the text. Another possible reading is that that the Hebrew conjunctive letter *vav* in verse three is more properly translated as "but" instead of "and", and if you ever learn Hebrew, one of the first things you'll learn is that "*vav*" can translate to either "and" or "but", depending on context *and or but or other things and it depends on the context and* flow of the passage to determine which it is. So in this case, it would actually be saying that Joash did was right in the sight of the Lord, except for, "but" he took two wives, and this would actually be a condemnation of the king's polygamous relationship, and it would concur with the law of Leviticus 18:18." –Aaron Ventura, pastor of Christ Covenant Church (CREC), Centralia, WA.

Everywhere in the Bible that polygamy is present, it is a snare and a destructive force. There are no positive examples. Kings are to represent God and are prohibited from multiple wives as reflections of Christ to avoid hearts turning from God. Paul gives us this same classification in Titus in regards to pastoral eldership.

Titus 1:5 For this reason I left you in Crete, that you would set in order what remains and appoint elders in every city as I directed you, 6 namely, if any man is above reproach, the **husband of one wife**, having children who believe, not accused of dissipation or rebellion. 7 For the overseer must be above reproach as God's steward, not **self-willed**, not quick-tempered, not addicted to wine, not pugnacious, not fond of sordid gain, 8 but hospitable, loving what is good, sensible, just, devout, self-controlled, 9 holding fast the faithful word which is in accordance with the teaching, so that he will be able both to exhort in sound doctrine and to refute those who contradict.

Look at that. This passage in Titus about Godly leadership mirrors the call to kings. All of the men who engaged in polygamy failed in their reigns and walks around the time when they were not husbands of one wife. Abraham went into Hagar in order to force the promise of God, and what was the result?

Genesis 16:2-3 So Sarai said to Abram, "Now behold, the Lord has prevented me from bearing children. Please go in to my maid; perhaps I will obtain children through her." And Abram listened to the voice of Sarai. 3 After Abram had lived ten years in the land of Canaan, Abram's wife Sarai took Hagar the

Egyptian, her maid, and gave her to her husband Abram as his
wife.

In this example, we have Abra(ha)m who is supposed to be waiting on
God to fulfill His promise. Abraham is supposed to be leading his wife.
Abraham should have led his wife to wait with him on the promises of
God in God's timing, as an example of the bride of Christ waiting on her
husband. Instead, Abraham acted like Adam in the garden and listened
to his wife's direction. At his wife's leadership, Abraham engaged in
polygamy. He did this while living in Canaan, and he took an Egyptian
woman—the two places mentioned as engaging in all forms of
forbidden relationships in Leviticus 18. What is the result of ignoring
God's timing and trying to force His promise?

> Genesis 16:5-6 And Sarai said to Abram, "May the wrong done
> me be upon you. I gave my maid into your arms, but when she
> saw that she had conceived, I was despised in her sight. May
> the Lord judge between you and me." 6 But Abram said to
> Sarai, "Behold, your maid is in your power; do to her what is
> good in your sight." So Sarai treated her harshly, and she fled
> from her presence.

Sarah afflicted her. One of the definitions is to bruise. This polygamous
relationship resulted in violence. Hagar ran away and God sent her back.
That wasn't the end of the division or contention in Abraham's house.

> Genesis 21:9-11 Now Sarah saw the son of Hagar the Egyptian,
> whom she had borne to Abraham, mocking. 10 Therefore she
> said to Abraham, "Drive out this maid and her son, for the son
> of this maid shall not be an heir with my son Isaac." 11 The
> matter distressed Abraham greatly because of his son.

188

Genesis 21: 14-17 So Abraham rose early in the morning and took bread and a skin of water and gave them to Hagar, putting them on her shoulder, and gave her the boy, <u>and sent her away</u>. And <u>she departed and wandered about in the wilderness of Beersheba.</u> 15 <u>When the water in the skin was used up, she left the boy under one of the bushes.</u> 16 Then she went and sat down opposite him, about a bowshot away, for she said, **<u>"Do not let me see the boy die</u>."** And she sat opposite him, and <u>lifted up her voice and wept</u>. 17 God heard the lad crying; and the angel of God called to Hagar from heaven and said to her, "What is the matter with you, Hagar? Do not fear, <u>for God has heard the voice of the lad where he is.</u>

The story of Abraham and Hagar is not a demonstration of God celebrating or even permitting polygamy. This is not what God's order and headship naturally results in. The laws governing polygamy in God's Law are not for endorsement of the practice, but for repentance. We are supposed to be a people who calls the world back to righteousness and walking in submission to God. In fact, to read Leviticus 18:18 as God permitting polygamy is to take the verse out of its meaning and context. Check this out:

> The legislation most frequently cited as support for polygamy and concubinage in the Pentateuch is found in Leviticus 18:18. This passage is commonly translated as tacitly allowing for plural marriages. For example, the NASB reads, "You shall not marry a woman in addition to her sister [Heb. 'ishah 'el-'akhotah, lit. 'a woman to her sister'] as a rival while she is alive, to uncover her nakedness." In this and most other modern versions, the phrase 'ishah 'el-'akhotah ("a woman to her

189

sister") is taken as referring to a literal (consanguine) sister. The implication of this reading is that although a certain incestuous polygamous relationship is forbidden (ie., marriage to two consanguine sisters while both are living, technically called sororal polygyny), polygamy in general is acceptable within the law. However, the Hebrew phrase 'ishah 'el-'akhotah ("a woman to her sister") in its eight occurrences elsewhere in the Hebrew Bible always is used idiomatically in the distributive sense of "one in addition to another," and nowhere refers to literal sisters.6 Likewise, the masculine equivalent of this phrase, 'ish 'el-'akiw ("a man to his brother"), appears twelve times in the Hebrew Bible, and is always used in a similar idiomatic manner with a distributive meaning of "one to another" or "to one another," and nowhere is it to be translated literally as "a man to his brother."7 Consistent with usage elsewhere in Scripture, Leviticus 18:18 should be taken idiomatically and distributively as referring to "one [woman/wife] in addition to another [woman/wife]," and not to literal sisters." –Davidson, Richard M., "Condemnation and Grace: Polygamy and Concubinage in the Old Testament" (2015). Faculty Publications. (69)

Is that not consistent with the rest of Scripture? Abraham vexed Sarah by listening to her council and taking another wife in addition to her. Consider yet another dynamic of prohibition of polygamy in the context that once a husband and wife become married, their is a naturalization of the family unit that occurs:

> *"This understanding of marriage is then confirmed by Leviticus 18:15, "You shall not uncover the nakedness of your daughter-in-*

law (כַּ.לָּ.תְ.ךָ); she is your son's wife, you shall not uncover her nakedness." <u>Because a man's wife has the status of an adopted sister, that man's father has to treat the woman as if she were his own "flesh of flesh" daughter.</u> In other words, <u>through marriage, husbands and wives share the same parents and can thus truly be considered adopted siblings.</u> This sheds light on a strange detail that pervades the Song of Songs, namely, the fact that Solomon keeps referring to his wife as his sister. Over and over again Solomon pours out his love for the woman he calls "my sister, my bride" (Song 4:9-10, 12, 5:1), even though we don't have a record of Solomon ever marrying one of his biological sisters. <u>In light of Scripture's teaching on adoption, it's most likely that Solomon's wife could be called his "sister" because of her marriage-adoption into Solomon's family.</u> This is further supported by the fact that the word translated as "bride" throughout the Song is "כַּ.לָּ.הּ," which is the very word used in Leviticus 18:15 to reference daughter-in-laws. <u>This strongly suggests that the Levitical understanding of marriage-adoption is at play here, demonstrating that, through marriage, the woman of the Song became the daughter of David, and the sister-bride of Solomon. All of this is crucial to understanding the only passage relevant to polygamy in Leviticus 18, "And you shall not take a woman as a rival wife to her sister, uncovering her nakedness while her sister is still alive"</u> (Lev. 18:18). Although the popular interpretation of this verse is that it only condemns polygamy with the biological sister of one's wife, we now know that it's doing much more than this. <u>Because marriage entails the status of an adopted sibling, if a man has two wives then these wives would always be sisters by virtue of</u>

*being married to the same man, and thereby sharing his father.
Leviticus 18:18 is thus a condemnation of polygamy as such,
which is why it refers to multiple sister-brides as "rivals" (צ ר ר).
An almost identical word is used in 1 Samuel 1:6 to describe how
Peninnah and Hannah were "rivals" (צ ר ה) due to their
mutual marriage to Elkanah, however it's never implied that
they were biological sisters. Instead, the reason two sister-brides
are rivals isn't due to their biological lineage, but rather their
marriage-adoption to the same man." – Codex Justinianeus,
scripture-forbids-polygamy/*

Where else can we see this dynamic of separate families becoming one
family? We see it in the genealogy of Christ. There is a recorded
genealogy of Christ through Joseph and though Joseph contributed no
genetic makeup to the creation of Christ, He is still regarded as if he had
and the account is listed in Matthew versus the genealogy through Mary
in Luke. This fusion of separate families becoming as one family is a
fascinating dynamic and bolsters the claim made regarding the
prohibition against polygamy. Furthermore, when we also see the case of
a widowed woman who has no children before her husband dies, then
the brother of the deceased husband is to give her a son so there may be
an heir and the name of the brother not be cut off before God, we can
see the naturalization of families in Scriptures.

Genesis 38:8 8 Then Judah said to Onan, "Go in to your
brother's wife, and perform your duty as a brother-in-law to
her, and raise up offspring for your brother."

The concept of naturalization in this way is how Ruth, who was a Moabitess, a people forbidden to enter into the assembly, is allowed to be part of Israel. Upon cleaving to God, Ruth was naturalized as an Israelite:

Ruth 1:16-18 But Ruth said, "Do not urge me to leave you or turn back from following you; for where you go, I will go, and where you lodge, I will lodge. Your people shall be my people, and your God, my God. 17 Where you die, I will die, and there I will be buried. Thus may the Lord do to me, and worse, if anything but death parts you and me." 18 When she saw that she was determined to go with her, she said no more to her.

Ephesians 2:11-14 Therefore remember that formerly you, the Gentiles in the flesh, who are called "Uncircumcision" by the so-called "Circumcision," which is performed in the flesh by human hands— 12 remember that you were at that time separate from Christ, excluded from the commonwealth of Israel, and strangers to the covenants of promise, having no hope and without God in the world. 13 But now in Christ Jesus you who formerly were far off have been brought near by the blood of Christ. 14 For He Himself is our peace, who made both groups into one and broke down the barrier of the dividing wall.

We see this process of familiar naturalization with gentiles into Israel, therefore it is reasonable to conclude that by marriage to the wife, the wife becomes a physical, natural daughter and taking another wife is to literally take a sister as a rival. Let's look at the Jacob matter. Jacob didn't seek to practice polygamy; it was an evil that was done to him by an evil man.

> Genesis 29:21 Then Jacob said to Laban, "Give me my wife, for my time is completed, that I may go in to her." 22 Laban gathered all the men of the place and made a feast. 23 Now in the evening <u>he took his daughter Leah, and brought her to him</u>; and Jacob went in to her. 24 Laban also gave his maid Zilpah to his daughter Leah as a maid. 25 <u>So it came about in the morning that, behold, it was Leah! And he said to Laban,</u> **"What is this you have done to me?** Was it not for Rachel that I served with you? **Why then have you deceived me?"** 26 But Laban said, "It is not the practice in our place to marry off the younger before the firstborn. 27 Complete the week of this one, and we will give you the other also for the service which you shall serve with me for another seven years."

Laban was a wicked man, emphasizing dominance over Jacob for profit and not in the ways of God. Laban was a diviner who engaged in wickedness.

> Genesis 30: But Laban said to him, "If now it pleases you, stay with me; <u>I have **divined**</u> that the Lord has blessed me on your account."

He was a man who served idols.

> Genesis 31:19 When Laban had gone to shear his flock, then <u>Rachel stole the household idols</u> that were her father's.

When Laban chased after Jacob in his departure, understanding that Jacob's leaving was by the hand of God, he makes him swear by the Name of God that Jacob won't take other wives:

> Genesis 31:50-53 <u>If you mistreat my daughters, or **if you take wives besides my daughters,** although no man is with us, see, God is witness between you and me.</u>" 51 Laban said to Jacob, "Behold this heap and behold the pillar which I have set between you and me. 52 This heap is a witness, and the pillar is a witness, that I will not pass by this heap to you for harm, and you will not pass by this heap and this pillar to me, for harm. 53 <u>The God of Abraham and the God of Nahor, the God of their father, judge between us."</u> So Jacob swore by the fear of his father Isaac.

I don't need to quote the entire story to you to show that the infighting, competing, and contentions between Rachel and Leah were not God's design for what a marriage is supposed to be. It certainly isn't a model for *our* marriage to Him as the bride of Christ.

> Proverbs 5:18-23 Let your fountain be blessed, And <u>rejoice in the **wife** of your youth.</u> 19 As a loving hind and a graceful doe, <u>Let **her** breasts satisfy you **at all times**;</u> Be <u>exhilarated **always with her** love.</u> 20 For <u>why should you, my son, be exhilarated with an adulteress And embrace the bosom of a foreigner?</u> 21 For <u>the ways of a man are before the eyes of the Lord, And He watches all his paths.</u> 22 His own iniquities will capture the wicked, And <u>he will be held with **the cords of his sin**.</u>23 <u>He</u>

will die for lack of instruction, And in the greatness of his folly he will go astray.

Did that say the harem of your youth? Did it say rejoice in the brothel of maidens that you have taken as wives? It does not. It's *one* wife, all one's days. Rejoice in your one wife. Be satisfied in her breasts. Not in several, not in many women's, but hers—your wife's. If you are satisfied with your wife at all times, as is this prescriptive command—you're not looking for another woman. If you're always exhilarated with her love, you're not looking for someone else's love. God is jealous for His bride, for our love and affection and attention. He doesn't take another, we're not supposed to either. When we take our eyes off of Him and our role in His leadership, in His dominion, as our Husband—then we seek carnality and we are led astray by the flesh and distort the image of God. We pervert every reflection of Him that He has made us to walk in.

2 Corinthians 11:2-3 For I am jealous for you with a godly jealousy; for I betrothed you to one husband, so that to Christ I might present you as a pure virgin. 3 But I am afraid that, as the serpent deceived Eve by his craftiness, your minds will be led astray from the simplicity and purity of devotion to Christ.

A husband who is looking for another wife in addition to the wife that he has is *not* a husband who is focused on loving his current wife like Christ loves the Church. He is not a husband who is focused on being the bride of Christ, but rather the exaltation of self.

Exodus 20:14 "You shall not commit adultery

Matthew 5:27-30 "You have heard that it was said, 'You shall not commit adultery'; 28 but I say to you **that everyone who looks at a woman with lust for her has already committed adultery with her in his heart.** 29 If your right eye makes you stumble, tear it out and throw it from you; for it is better for you to lose one of the parts of your body, than for your whole body to be thrown into hell. 30 If your right hand makes you stumble, cut it off and throw it from you; for it is better for you to lose one of the parts of your body, than for your whole body to go into hell.

Looking at a woman with lust is adultery. Looking at someone with lust who is not your wife is adultery. This does *not* say "if your eye causes you to sin, just sin bro—it's fine" or, "There are laws that regulate sin, therefore God is pleased if I go choose sin". That would be a justification for flesh. That would be blasphemous. The imagery of severance from the body is so strong and severe here for a reason. We're told throughout Scripture that our focus is to be on God.

Matthew 6:31-33 Do not worry then, saying, 'What will we eat?' or 'What will we drink?' or 'What will we wear for clothing?' 32 For the Gentiles eagerly seek all these things; for your heavenly Father knows that you need all these things. 33 **But seek first His kingdom and His righteousness,** and all these things will be added to you.

Just like God said with David, *if* there was a need for multiple wives, He would have made it so. He forbids it, and therefore it is not so. The greatest commands from God are to love God with all your heart and to love your neighbor as yourself. Loving God with all your heart is submission to His leadership and dominion and loving one spouse the way He tells us to.

> Revelation 19:7-9 Let <u>us rejoice and be glad and give the glory to Him, for</u> <u>the marriage of the Lamb has come</u> and **His bride has made herself ready.**" 8 It was given <u>to her to clothe herself in fine linen, bright and clean;</u> for the fine linen is the righteous acts of the saints.9 Then he *said to me, "Write, 'Blessed are those who are invited to the marriage supper of the Lamb.'" And he *said to me, "These are true words of God."

One Bride. Just like the Messiah only has one Bride.

Now those who advocate for multiple wives will likely read this statement and say "God doesn't have only one bride, He talks about two, Israel and Judah, and being as a husband to both." That analogy to depict a concept is used in Scripture, and when we reconcile it with the rest of the passages, we see that we become united as *one*:

> Ezekiel 37:15-28 The word of the Lord came again to me saying, 16 "And you, son of man, take for yourself one stick and write on it, 'For Judah and for the sons of Israel, his companions'; then take another stick and write on it, 'For Joseph, the stick of Ephraim and all the house of Israel, his companions.' 17 Then join them for yourself one to another into one stick<u>, that they may become one in your hand</u>. 18 When the sons of your people speak to you saying, 'Will you not declare to us what you mean by these?' 19 say to them, 'Thus says the Lord God, "Behold, I will take the stick of Joseph, which is in the hand of Ephraim, and the tribes of Israel, his companions; and I will put them with it, with the

stick of Judah<u>, and make them one stick, and they will be one</u> <u>in My hand.</u>'" 20 The sticks on which you write will be in your hand before their eyes. 21 Say to them, 'Thus says the Lord God, <u>"Behold, I will take the sons of Israel from among the</u> <u>nations where they have gone, and I will gather them from</u> <u>every side and bring them into their own land; 22 and I will</u> <u>make them one nation in the land, on the mountains of Israel;</u> <u>and one king will be king for all of them; and they will no</u> <u>longer be two nations and no longer be divided into two</u> <u>kingdoms.</u>

Just as Deuteronomy 17:17 states that a King is not to have multiple wives, our example of God as a husband—Christ, who gave that law— only has one bride.

CHAPTER ELEVEN

The Restoration of God's Dominion

> Ephesians 5:7 that <u>He might present to Himself the church in all her glory, having no spot or wrinkle</u> or any such thing; <u>but that she would be holy and blameless.</u>

We're told throughout Scripture that our focus is to be on God. We can't walk in rebellion *and* submission at the same time. We can't walk in fear and faith at the same time.

> Matthew 6:31-33 Do not worry then, saying, 'What will we eat?' or 'What will we drink?' or 'What will we wear for clothing?' 32 For the Gentiles eagerly seek all these things; for your heavenly Father knows that you need all these things. 33 **But seek first His kingdom and His righteousness,** and all these things will be added to you.

The greatest commands from God are to love God with all your heart and to love your neighbor as yourself.

> Matthew 22:36-40 <u>"Teacher, which is the great commandment in the Law?"</u> 37 And He said to him, "**You shall love the Lord your God with all your heart, and with all your soul, and with all your mind.'** 38 This is the great and foremost commandment. 39 **The second is like it, 'You**

shall love your neighbor as yourself.' 40 On these two commandments depend the whole Law and the Prophets.".

Christ is telling people to follow the Law. He's instructing the Biblical order and submission to God. Christ is establishing that the first and greatest point is that we, as the bride, submit to our Husband. The second is to love others. He's quoting the Law itself.

Deuteronomy 6:5 **You shall love the Lord your God with all your heart and with all your soul and with all your might**.

Leviticus 19:18 You shall not take vengeance, nor bear any grudge against the sons of your people, **but you shall love your neighbor as yourself**; I am the Lord.

Our world is in such a fallen and disordered state because of these not being followed. As a culture, we champion rebellion against God's order. As a society, we contextualize marriage as a burdensome matter. When our culture does praise marriage, it's too often when there is a distortion of God's order. Children are raised observing models in their parents of contention instead of love, solidarity, unity, and self-sacrifice. They grow up to be adults who foster hyper-liberalism. The lessons shift from "love your neighbor as yourself" to "reject everything that doesn't serve you," which is the opposite of sacrifice. Mankind emulates that which he focuses on. If we are looking at God and the things of God, we emulate God and build the kingdom of God. When we focus on ourselves, we become a recursive echo of flesh, desire, and the lusts of the world.

How do we return to His righteous dominion? We repent. We acknowledge that our ways are not His ways. We seek *His* heart and *His* ways. Not in a legal box checking list of dos and don'ts, but in right relationship out of love for God and a naturally inspired desire to do good to one you love.

> Isaiah 55:6-9 <u>Seek the Lord while He may be found; Call upon Him while He is near. 7 Let the wicked forsake his way</u> And <u>the unrighteous man his thoughts; And let him return to the Lord</u>, And He will have compassion on him, And to our God, For He will abundantly pardon. 8 "<u>For My thoughts are not your thoughts, Nor are your ways My ways</u>," declares the Lord. 9 "For as the heavens are higher than the earth, <u>So are My ways higher than your ways And My thoughts than your thoughts.</u>

Our ways are violence, hate, destruction, and fleshly darkness. His ways are peace, life, joy, forgiveness, prosperity, and cultivation. When we stand against Him in our insistent ways, we're not reflecting God's glory, we're depicting the adversary.

> Daniel 7: 25-27 <u>He will speak out against the Most High</u> and <u>wear down the saints of the Highest One</u>, and <u>he will intend to make alterations in times and in law</u>; and they will be given into his hand for a time, times, and half a time. 26 **But the court will sit for judgment, and his dominion will be taken away, annihilated and destroyed forever**. 27 Then <u>the sovereignty, the dominion and the greatness of all the kingdoms under the whole heaven will be given to the people</u>

of the saints of the Highest One; <u>His kingdom will be an everlasting kingdom, and **all the dominions will serve and obey Him.'**</u>

This is what happens. He *is* King of Kings and Lord of Lords, and when we choose to stand against His dominion and oppose his Law, there isn't a heaven that we enter. Heaven is a place for those who love, and honor, and obey Him.

Revelation 21:1-8 Then <u>I saw a new heaven and a new earth;</u> for <u>the first heaven and the first earth passed away, and there is no longer any sea.</u> 2 And I saw the holy city, new Jerusalem, **coming down out of heaven from God, made ready <u>as a bride adorned for her husband.</u>** 3 And I heard a loud voice from the throne, saying, "Behold, the tabernacle of God is among men, and <u>He will dwell among them, and they shall be His people, and God Himself will be among them</u>, 4 and He will wipe away every tear from their eyes; and there will no longer be any death; there will no longer be any mourning, or crying, or pain; the first things have passed away."

5 And **He who sits on the throne said, "Behold, I am making all things new."** And He *said, "Write, for these words are faithful and true." 6 Then He said to me, "It is done. I am the Alpha and the Omega, the beginning and the end. <u>I will give to the one who thirsts from the spring of the water of life without cost. 7 He who overcomes will inherit these things, and I will be his God **and he will be My son.**</u> 8 But for <u>the cowardly and unbelieving and abominable and murderers and immoral persons and sorcerers and idolaters and all liars, their</u>

part will be in the lake that burns with fire and brimstone, which is the second death."

Do you see that contrast? The obedient will be sons of God, but the violent, immoral, sorcerers, idolaters, and liars—those who are Nephilim—they will be destroyed.

> Luke 17:26-37 And just as it happened in the days of Noah, so it will be also in the days of the Son of Man: 27 they were eating, they were drinking, they were marrying, they were being given in marriage, until the day that Noah entered the ark, and the flood came and destroyed them all. 28 It was the same as happened in the days of Lot: they were eating, they were drinking, they were buying, they were selling, they were planting, they were building; 29 but on the day that Lot went out from Sodom it rained fire and brimstone from heaven and destroyed them all. 30 It will be just the same on the day that the Son of Man is revealed. 31 On that day, the one who is on the housetop and whose goods are in the house must not go down to take them out; and likewise the one who is in the field must not turn back. 32 Remember Lot's wife. 33 Whoever seeks to keep his life will lose it, and whoever loses his life will preserve it. 34 I tell you, on that night there will be two in one bed; one will be taken and the other will be left. 35 There will be two women grinding at the same place; one will be taken and the other will be left. 36 [Two men will be in the field; one will be taken and the other will be left."] 37 And answering they *said to Him, "Where, Lord?" And He said to them, "Where the body is, there also the vultures will be gathered."

Judgment day is going to be like the days of Noah. Sons of God walking in obedience versus those who are engaged in wickedness. This prophecy found in Isaiah 66 about the end times tells us much about what to expect.

> Isaiah 66:1-3 Thus says the Lord,
> "Heaven is My throne and the earth is My footstool.
> Where then is a house you could build for Me?
> And where is a place that I may rest?
> 2 <u>"For My hand made all these things,</u>
> <u>Thus all these things came into being," declares the Lord.</u>
> "But to **this one** I will look,
> <u>To him who is humble and contrite of spirit, and who</u>
> <u>trembles at My word.</u>

God made all things and He looks for those who are humble and follow His word.

> Isaiah 66:3-4 "But he who kills an ox is like one who slays a man;
> He who sacrifices a lamb is like the one who breaks a dog's neck;
> He who offers a grain offering is like one who offers swine's blood;
> He who burns incense is like the one who blesses an idol.
> <u>As **they have chosen their own ways,**</u>
> <u>And **their soul delights in their abominations,**</u>
> 4 So I will choose their punishments
> And will bring on them what they dread.
> <u>Because I called, but no one answered;</u>
> <u>I spoke, but they did not listen.</u>
> <u>And they did evil in My sight</u>
> <u>And chose that in which I did not delight."</u>

Those who think that they can trample the grace of God and put forth offerings while loving their sins and rebellions will have their offerings rejected. Those who love sin and think that just because they call themselves believers that God is pleased when they walk and persist in contrary ways are in for a very harsh awakening at His return.

> Isaiah 66:5-6 Hear the word of the Lord, <u>you who tremble at His word</u>:
> <u>"Your brothers</u> **who hate you, who exclude you for My name's sake,**
> <u>Have said, 'Let the Lord be glorified, that we may see your joy.'</u>
> But **they will be put to shame**.
> 6 <u>"A voice of uproar from the city, a voice from the temple,</u>
> <u>The voice of the Lord who is rendering recompense to His enemies.</u>

Those who hold to the Word are offensive to those who do not. John 16:1-3 emphasizes this point:

> John 16:1-3"These things I have spoken to you so that you may be kept from stumbling. 2 <u>They will make you outcasts from the synagogue,</u> but an hour is coming <u>for everyone who kills you to think that he is offering service to God.</u> 3 **These things they will do because they have not known the Father or Me.**

Discernment again. The difference between right, and *almost* right.

Isaiah 66:7- 14"Before she travailed, she brought forth;
<u>Before her pain came, she gave birth to a boy.</u>
8 "Who has heard such a thing? Who has seen such things?
Can a land be born in one day?
Can a nation be brought forth all at once?
As soon as Zion travailed, she also brought forth her sons.
9 "<u>Shall I bring to the point of birth and not give delivery?</u>" says the Lord.
"<u>Or shall I who gives delivery shut the womb?</u>" says your God.
10 "Be joyful with Jerusalem and rejoice for her, all you who love her;
Be exceedingly glad with her, all you who mourn over her,
11 That <u>you may nurse and be satisfied</u> with her comforting breasts,
That you may suck and be delighted with her bountiful bosom."
12 For thus says the Lord, "Behold, I extend peace to her like a river,
And the glory of the nations like an overflowing stream;
And <u>you will be nursed, you will be carried on the hip and fondled on the knees.</u>
13 "<u>As one whom his mother comforts, so I will comfort you;</u>
And you will be comforted in Jerusalem."
14 Then you will see this, and your heart will be glad,
And your bones will flourish like the new grass;
And <u>the hand of the Lord will be made known to His servants,</u>
But He will be indignant toward His enemies.

The language is that we will be sons of God, children of God, nursed by Jerusalem where He sets His Name. Though we have enemies and those who walk contrary to His ways and reject His authority and dominion—even while professing to be His followers, He will still preserve His remnant and those who love Him as a parent.

Isaiah 66:15-17 <u>For behold, the Lord will come in fire</u>
<u>And His chariots like the whirlwind,</u>
<u>To render His anger with fury,</u>
<u>And His rebuke with flames of fire.</u>
16 For <u>the Lord will execute judgment by fire</u>
<u>And by His sword on all flesh,</u>
<u>And those slain by the Lord will be many.</u>
17 "Those who sanctify and purify themselves to go to the gardens,
Following one in the center,
<u>Who eat swine's flesh, detestable things and mice,</u>
<u>Will come to an end altogether,</u>" declares the Lord.

God is telling us clearly that at the second coming when He comes with His fire and His angels that those slain will be many, those who are against His laws and dominion and rule, specifically mentioning those who profess that eating unclean animals is something that God says is acceptable. Swine's flesh and mice being eaten are a provocation to God, so why should we misinterpret that He has made eating them no longer a sin? Why would God change one sin to not being a sin in order to pander to the tastes and flesh-based passions of people? He doesn't. He didn't. He won't.

Isaiah 66:18-24 "For **I know their works and their thoughts**; the time is coming to gather all nations and tongues. And they shall come and see My glory. 19 I will set a sign among them and will send survivors from them to the nations: Tarshish, Put, Lud, Meshech, Tubal and Javan, to the distant coastlands that have neither heard My fame nor seen My glory. And they will declare My glory among the nations. 20 Then they shall bring all your brethren from all the nations as a grain offering to the Lord, on horses, in chariots, in litters, on mules and on camels, to My holy mountain Jerusalem," says the Lord, "just as the sons of Israel bring their grain offering in a clean vessel to the house of the Lord. 21 I will also take some of them for priests and for Levites," says the Lord. 22 "For just as the new heavens and the new earth which I make will endure before Me," declares the Lord, "So your offspring and your name will endure. 23 **And it shall be from new moon to new moon and from sabbath to sabbath, all mankind will come to bow down before Me,**" says the Lord. 24 "**Then they will go forth and look on the corpses of the men who have transgressed against Me. For their worm will not die and their fire will not be quenched; And they will be an abhorrence to all mankind.**"'

There will be judgment and at the return of Christ, He is going to take for Himself Levites and priests. The inhabitants of the new heaven and new earth are going to be keeping Holy Days and the Law of God. God established them from the beginning and they are there at the end. This may be rudimentary, but the reason that there are winter gaps in the Holy times is because all of the feasts parallel the seasons.

Jeremiah 8:20"Harvest is past, summer is ended, And we are not saved."

Meaning that from the beginning, we have time for growth and labor, but in the end, there will be death and destruction—and only the fruit of our labor will remain.

> John 4::34-36 " Jesus *said to them, "<u>My food is to do the will of Him who sent Me and to accomplish His work</u>. 35 Do you not say, <u>'There are yet four months, and then comes the harvest'</u>? Behold, I say to you, <u>lift up your eyes and look on the fields, that they are white for harvest</u>. 36 Already he who reaps is receiving wages <u>and is gathering fruit for life eternal; so that he who sows and he who reaps may rejoice together</u>.

The seasons themselves are a testament of the gospel, that death/winter is coming for us all, but faithfulness and obedience in Christ will allow us to stand in the end. We are laborers in the field, in the harvest, and at the end of the harvest- the separation of the wheat and the chaff and the tares. Maybe you've never heard or understood these things before, but we are supposed to be keeping the feasts and obeying God now, not out of hard-hearted resentment but out of love for God. Every feast is an expression of God's love and our love for God. Let's walk through a few of them and what they stand for.

> Leviticus 23:2 "Speak to the sons of Israel and say to them, '<u>The Lord's appointed times</u> which <u>you shall proclaim as holy convocations</u>—**My appointed times** are these:

Remember whose times they are: the Lord's appointed times. What are we supposed to do? Proclaim them as holy convocations. His appointed times.

Leviticus 23: 3 'For six days work may be done, but on the seventh day there is a sabbath of complete rest, a holy convocation. You shall not do any work; it is a sabbath to the Lord in all your dwellings.

Exodus 20 has a fuller expounding of the commandment:

Exodus 20:811 "Remember **the** sabbath day, to keep **it** holy. 9 Six days you shall labor and do all your work, 10 but the seventh day is a sabbath of the Lord your God; in it you shall not do any work, you or your son or your daughter, your male or your female servant or your cattle or your sojourner who stays with you. 11 For in six days the Lord made the heavens and the earth, the sea and all that is in them, and rested on the seventh day; therefore the Lord **blessed the sabbath** day and made **it** holy.

There are some people who suggest that any day can be the sabbath of their choosing, or rather, because the sabbath was made for man, they don't have to rest the way God commands. Does that verse say that the Sabbath is only for man, though? Does it not say that it's also for the cattle? Even the land has sabbaths. It's a holy rest not only for Man, but everything under man's dominion. There are others who tend to say that the Sabbath is only for the Jews, but does it not say that it's for the sojourner too?

Deuteronomy 5:21 'You shall not covet your neighbor's wife, and you shall not desire your neighbor's house, his field or his male servant or his female servant, his ox or his donkey or anything that belongs to your neighbor.'

Pro-nomian Pastor Joshua Ensley makes this excellent point:

> "Both marriage and the Sabbath were ordained at creation. If
> we were to argue that the Sabbath is just a temporary statute
> just for the Jews, we must logically extend that reasoning to say
> that Marriage, too, is just a temporary statute for the Jews" –
> Joshua Ensley *via Social media X.com*

Have you noticed that the commandment on keeping the Sabbath is
similar to the command against coveting, as we're not to covet another
man's wife, house, field, or animals? We wouldn't look at this and say
something silly like, "Those commands against coveting are only for the
Jews". God intended this for everyone. The Sabbath is a gift for
everyone. Remember being a kid and your parents trying to get you to
take a nap because you were getting cranky and maybe you might have
developed a little bit of an attitude with them? That's right from God,
probably. I can see God looking at us, His children, and seeing how we'd
push ourselves trying to fight order and trying to do everything in our
strength and our power, and Him saying, "Listen, why don't you get
some rest". Remember how we used to fight that nap as children, but as
adults we think back at how silly that was because naps are awesome?
People do that same thing with the Sabbath for some reason. A husband
who cares for his wife and sees her doing too much will tell his wife that
she needs to come sit down with him and relax. If that is a clear example
of love in a healthy relationship, why would we fight that when God
says it to us? Loving parents want what is best for us; God does too!

There are other people, like the rabbis and the Pharisees, who have many particular traditions and commandments of men that they follow in how they choose to keep the sabbath. That's fine if they want to do that. Each person is encouraged to look at the Scriptures and work out their convictions in matters that are not expressly outlined in the Word. I don't have to do it that way. I have to obey what is in the parameters of Scripture. There is nothing in the Bible that says that you can't tear toilet paper, have your pre-paid electricity on, or write notes down as you're reading your Bible. How do you keep the Sabbath holy? You stop working, you, your house, your people that work for you, and your animals. You don't go about advancing your business and insisting on your own means that are contrary to what God is wanting, and you rest. Sleep in. Eat something fancy you bought for the Sabbath in anticipation of its arrival. Rejoice in the presence of God as you would a new wife basking in the presence of her new husband. Christ says His yolk is easy and His burden is light. The things of God only seem hard at first because our flesh is so hostile to them. We are to gather with other believers in a holy assembly to worship and glorify God as one body on the day He expressly sets apart.

So what does the Sabbath teach us?

> Luke 4:16 And He came to Nazareth, where He had been brought up; and <u>as was His custom, He entered the synagogue on the Sabbath</u>, and stood up to read.

The first thing it teaches us is how to live like Christ. It teaches us that our way, our dominion, is in submission to His. It teaches us that we are not the ones in control. We're not fighting God for headship and authority when we're keeping the Sabbath. We're not pretending that we're honoring Him by taking His Sabbath that He set and rescheduling it. I have heard it said that there is no New Testament command for us to keep the Sabbath. Is that true though? Does Hebrews 4 say this? There are many people who read Hebrews 4 and try to render it into a vague concept of the sabbath rather than its reading that says that to not enter into that rest is disobedience.

Ezekiel 20: 8-24 Then I resolved to pour out My wrath on them, to accomplish My anger against them in the midst of the land of Egypt. 9 But I acted for the sake of My name, that it should not be profaned in the sight of the nations among whom they lived, in whose sight I made Myself known to them by bringing them out of the land of Egypt. 10 So I took them out of the land of Egypt and brought them into the wilderness. 11 I gave them My statutes and informed them of My ordinances, by which, if a man observes them, he will live. 12 **Also I gave them My sabbaths to be a sign between Me and them, that they might know that I am the Lord who sanctifies them.** 13 But the house of Israel rebelled against Me in the wilderness. They did not walk in My statutes and they rejected My ordinances, by which, if a man observes them, he will live; and **My sabbaths they greatly profaned. Then I resolved to pour out My wrath on them in the wilderness, to annihilate them.** 14 But I acted for the sake of My name, that it should not be profaned in the sight of the nations, before whose sight I had brought them out. 15 Also I swore to them in the wilderness that I would not bring them into the land which I had given them, flowing with milk and honey, which is the glory of all lands, 16 **because they rejected My ordinances, and as for My statutes, they did not walk in them; they even profaned My sabbaths, for their heart continually went after their idols.** 17 Yet My eye spared them rather than destroying them, and I did not cause their annihilation in the wilderness. 18 "I said to their children in the wilderness, **'Do not walk in the statutes of your fathers or keep their ordinances or defile yourselves with their idols. 19 I am the Lord your God; walk in My statutes and keep My ordinances and observe them. 20 Sanctify My sabbaths; and they shall be a sign between Me and you, that you may know that I am the Lord your God.' 21 But the children rebelled against Me; they did not walk in My statutes, nor were they careful to observe My ordinances, by which, if a man observes them, he will live; they profaned My sabbaths. So I resolved to pour out My wrath on them, to accomplish My anger against them in the wilderness.** 22 But I withdrew My hand and acted for the sake of My name, that it should not be profaned in the sight of the nations in whose sight I had brought them out. 23 Also I swore to them in the wilderness that I would scatter them among the nations and disperse them among the lands, **24 because they had not observed My ordinances, but had rejected My statutes and had profaned My sabbaths, and their eyes were on the idols of their fathers.**

Let's look at the comparisons:

Hebrews 4:1-16 Therefore, since the promise of entering his rest still stands, <u>let us be careful that none of you be found to have fallen short of it</u>. 2 For we also have had the good news proclaimed to us, just as they did; but the message they heard was of no value to them, **because they did not share the faith of those who obeyed**. 3 Now we who have believed enter that rest, just as God has said, "So I declared an oath in my anger, 'They shall never enter my rest.'" "And yet <u>his works have been finished since the creation of the world.</u> 4 For somewhere he has spoken about the seventh day in these words: **"On the seventh day YHWH rested from all his works."** 5 And again in the passage above he says, "They shall never enter my rest." 6 Therefore since it still remains for some to enter that rest, <u>and since those who formerly had the good news proclaimed to them did not go in because of their disobedience</u>, 7 YHWH again set a certain day, calling it "Today." This he did when a long time later he spoke through David, as in the passage already quoted: "Today, if you hear his voice, do not harden your hearts." 8 For if Joshua had given them rest, God would not have spoken later about another day. 9 **There remains, then, a Sabbath-rest for the people of God; 10 for anyone who enters God's rest also rests from their works, <u>just as God did from his</u>. 11 Let us, therefore, make every effort to enter that rest, so that no one will perish by following their example of disobedience**. 12 For the word of YHWH is alive and active. Sharper than any double-edged sword, it penetrates even to dividing soul and spirit, joints and marrow; it judges the thoughts and attitudes of the heart. 13 Nothing in all creation is hidden from God's sight. Everything is uncovered and laid bare before the eyes of him to whom we must give account.14 Therefore, since we have a great high priest who has ascended into heaven, Yahshua the Son of God, let us hold firmly to the faith we profess. 15 For we do not have a high priest who is unable to empathize with our weaknesses, but we have one who has been tempted in every way, just as we are—yet he did not sin. 16 Let us then approach YHWH's throne of grace with confidence, so that we may receive mercy and find grace to help us in our time of need.

The parallel of Ezekiel in Hebrews 4 showcases that Hebrews 4 is *affirming* the Sabbath and ordinances of God *are* to be kept in actuality. They are practical and physical commands to rest and walk in His ways. We submit to His order when we keep His sabbath. We're not pretending that we're the ones who provide for ourselves.

> Isaiah 58:13-14 "If because of the sabbath, you turn your foot From doing your own pleasure on My holy day,
> And call the sabbath a delight, **the holy day of the Lord** honorable, And honor it, desisting from your own ways, From seeking your own pleasure And speaking your own word, 14 Then you will take delight in the Lord, And I will make you ride on the heights of the earth; And I will feed you with the heritage of Jacob your father, For the mouth of the Lord has spoken."

When it says don't do your own pleasure, it's agreed by numerous scholars that the interpretation of that passage is to not engage in commerce by selling or buying goods or conducting any kind of business. The prophet Nehemiah gives clarity:

Nehemiah 13:15-22 In those days I saw in Judah some who were <u>treading wine presses on the sabbath</u>, and <u>bringing in sacks of grain</u> and <u>loading them on donkeys</u>, as well as wine, grapes, figs and <u>all kinds of loads</u>, and <u>they brought them into Jerusalem on the sabbath day</u>. So I admonished them on the day they sold food. 16 Also men of Tyre were living there who imported fish and all kinds of merchandise<u>, and sold them to the sons of Judah on the sabbath</u>, even in Jerusalem. 17 Then I reprimanded the nobles of Judah and said to them, "<u>What is this evil thing you are doing, by profaning the sabbath day</u>? 18 <u>Did not your fathers do the same</u>, so that our God brought on us and on this city all this trouble? <u>Yet you are adding to the wrath on Israel by profaning the sabbath.</u>"
19 It came about that just as it grew dark at the gates of Jerusalem before the sabbath, I commanded that the doors should be shut and that they should not open them until after the sabbath. Then I stationed some of my servants at the gates so that no load would enter on the sabbath day. 20 Once or twice the traders and merchants of every kind of merchandise spent the night outside Jerusalem. 21 Then I warned them and said to them, "Why do you spend the night in front of the wall? If you do so again, I will use force against you." From that time on they did not come on the sabbath. 22 <u>And I commanded the Levites that they should purify themselves and come as gatekeepers to sanctify the sabbath day.</u> For this

also remember me, O my God, and have compassion on me according to the greatness of Your lovingkindness."

Your focus shouldn't be on getting your household chores done or buying the things you want to buy. It should be on God and delighting in His presence. This is sometimes framed as legalism, but is not cheating on your wife legalism? Is not murdering your brother in a field legalism? No way. They are the things you do because you have love in your heart. Sabbath commands are not boxes you check, they are romantic gestures for the relationship you hold with the Creator of heaven and earth.

> Leviticus 23:4-8 'These are the appointed times of the Lord, holy convocations which you shall proclaim at the times appointed for them. 5 In the first month, on the fourteenth day of the month at twilight is the Lord's Passover. 6 Then on the fifteenth day of the same month there is the Feast of Unleavened Bread to the Lord; for seven days you shall eat unleavened bread. 7 On the first day you shall have a holy convocation; you shall not do any laborious work. 8 But for seven days you shall present an offering by fire to the Lord. On the seventh day is a holy convocation; you shall not do any laborious work.'"

Sweet, two days off in one week. Let's look at the Passover and what does this teach us?

> 1 Corinthians 5 :6-8 Your boasting is not good. Do you not know that a little leaven leavens the whole lump of dough? 7

> Clean out the old leaven so that you may be a new lump, just as
> you are in fact unleavened. For **Christ our Passover** also **has
> been sacrificed**. 8 Therefore **let us celebrate the feast**, not
> with old leaven, nor with the leaven of malice and wickedness,
> but with **the unleavened bread of sincerity and truth**.

Paul is telling us that Christ is our Passover Lamb, and that we should be
keeping the Passover, clearing out sin, which is symbolized in leaven. It's
about being as unleavened bread in sincerity and truth.

> Exodus 12: 3-4 Speak to all the congregation of Israel, saying,
> 'On the tenth of this month they are each one to take a lamb
> for themselves, according to their fathers' households, a lamb
> for each household. 4 Now if the household is too small for a
> lamb, then he and his neighbor nearest to his house are to take
> one according to the number of persons in them; according to
> what each man should eat, you are to divide the lamb

It started with a selection of lamb, and how we are to eat it.

> John 6:53 So Jesus said to them, "Truly, truly, I say to you,
> **unless you eat the flesh of the Son of Man and drink His
> blood, you have no life in yourselves.**

Christ is telling them that *He* is the Passover Lamb that is slain. We are
to partake of *Him* for eternal life in obedience to the commands of God.

> Exodus 12: 5 **Your lamb shall be an unblemished male** a
> year old; you may take it from the sheep or from the goats.

We see Peter making the parallel in 1 Peter:

1 Peter 1:18 - 19 knowing that <u>you were not redeemed with perishable things </u>like silver or gold **from your futile way of life inherited from your forefathers**, 19 **but with precious blood, as of a lamb unblemished and spotless, the blood of Christ**.

It was both personal and corporate for the congregation.

Exodus 12:6 You shall keep it until the fourteenth day of the same month, then **<u>the whole assembly</u>** <u>of the congregation of Israel is to</u> **kill it at twilight**.

Matthew 27:24 When Pilate saw that he was accomplishing nothing, but rather that a riot was starting, he took water and washed his hands in front of the crowd, saying, "I am innocent of this Man's blood; see to that yourselves." 25 **<u>And all the people</u>** <u>said, "His blood shall be on us and on our children!"</u>

Luke 23: 44-46 <u>It was now about the sixth hour, and darkness fell over the whole land</u> **until the ninth hour** , 45 <u>because the sun was obscured; and the veil of the temple was torn in two.</u> 46 And Jesus, crying out with a loud voice, said, "Father, into Your hands I commit My spirit." Having said this, He breathed His last.

"From the ninth (three o'clock) to the 11th hour" (five o'clock). The ancient **custom was to slay the Passover shortly after the daily sacrifice, i.e. three o'clock, with which hour Christ's death coincided**. – A.R. Fausset, Bible dictionary; Passover–citing Josephus (B. J., 6:9, section 3)

The Restoration of God's Dominion

Philo, a famous Jewish philosopher of Alexandria born in 25 B.C., had this to say about the sacrifices:

> For some of them are offered up every day, and some on the days of the new moon, and at the festivals of the full moon; others on days of fasting; and others at three different occasions of festival. Accordingly, it is commanded that every day the priests should offer up two lambs, one at the dawn of day, and the other in the evening; each of them being a sacrifice of thanksgiving; the one for the kindnesses which have been bestowed during the day, and the other **for the mercies** which have been vouchsafed in the night, **which God is incessantly and uninterruptedly pouring upon the race of men**. – Philo, *Special Laws* I, XXXV (169) Philo of Alexandria (a.k.a. Philo Judaeus, ca. 15 BCE–50 CE)

God made the day dark as the mercy sacrifice of Christ was presented for all of mankind in that He died in our place for our sins.

> Exodus 12:8-11 They shall eat the flesh that same night, roasted with fire, and they shall eat it with unleavened bread and bitter herbs.9 Do not eat any of it raw or boiled at all with water, but rather roasted with fire, both its head and its legs along with its entrails. 10 And you shall not leave any of it over until morning, but whatever is left of it until morning, you shall burn with fire.11 Now you shall eat it in this manner: with your loins girded, your sandals on your feet, and your staff in your hand; and you shall eat it in haste—**it is the Lord's Passover.**

Note that it is not to be left overnight. We see that there were righteous men who went to make sure that Christ was not left on the cross overnight, as the command states.

> Luke 23:50-56 And a man named Joseph, who was a member of the Council, a good and righteous man 51 (he had not consented to their plan and action), a man from Arimathea, a city of the Jews, who was waiting for the kingdom of God; 52 this man went to Pilate and asked for the body of Jesus. 53 And he took it down and wrapped it in a linen cloth, and laid Him in a tomb cut into the rock, where no one had ever lain. 54 It was the preparation day, and the Sabbath was about to begin. 55 Now the women who had come with Him out of Galilee followed, and saw the tomb and how His body was laid. 56 Then they returned and prepared spices and perfumes. **And on the Sabbath they rested according to the commandment**.

Notice that they rested according to the commandment. It says that it is the Lord's Passover, not the Passover of the Jews. Christ is the offering for all, Jew and non-Jew.

> Exodus 12:12-13 For I will go through the land of Egypt on that night, and will strike down all the firstborn in the land of Egypt, both man and beast; and against all the gods of Egypt I will execute judgments—I am the Lord. 13 **The blood shall be a sign for you on the houses where you live; and when I see the blood I will pass over you,** and no plague will befall you to destroy you when I strike the land of Egypt.

Hebrews 9:14 how much more will <u>the blood of Christ</u>, who through the eternal Spirit <u>offered Himself without blemish to God</u>, cleanse your conscience <u>from dead works to serve the living God</u>?

Acts 16:31-34 They said, "<u>Believe in the Lord Jesus, and you will be saved</u>, **you and your household**." 32 And they spoke the word of the Lord to him together **with all who were in his house**. 33 And he took them that very hour of the night and washed their wounds, and **immediately he was baptized, he and all his household.** 34 And he brought them into his house and set food before them, and rejoiced greatly, **having believed in God with his whole household.**

Christ's blood is the means of our salvation, which is placed on the doorposts of our hearts, that we might live and have eternal life.

Exodus 12:14 'Now this day will be a memorial to you, and you shall celebrate it as a feast to the Lord; <u>throughout your generations</u> you are to **celebrate it as a permanent ordinance**.

A permanent ordinance literally means forever, always, continuous existence, perpetual, everlasting, indefinite, unending future, or eternity. This is something that *hasn't* been done away with. We could even make the strong case that when Christ says, "Do this in remembrance of Me," He's re-emphasizing that *He* is the Passover and that we are to still be obedient.

Exodus 12:15 Seven days you shall eat unleavened bread, <u>but on the first day you shall remove leaven from your houses</u>; for whoever eats anything leavened from the first day until the seventh day**, that person shall be cut off from Israel.**

What does that teach us about Christ and God's dominion? It teaches us that leaven represents sin. It teaches us that we are to remove sin from our lives and live like Christ. Deuteronomy 31:11-13 gives a breakdown of who Israel is:

Deuteronomy 31:11-13 When <u>all Israel</u> comes to appear before the Lord your God at the place which He will choose, you shall read this law in front of <u>all Israel</u> in their hearing. 12 Assemble the people,<u> the</u> **men** <u>and the</u> **women** <u>and</u> **children** <u>and</u> **the alien** <u>who is in your town, so that</u> <u>they may hear and learn and fear the Lord your God, and be careful to observe all the words of this law</u>. 13 **Their children, who have not known, will hear and learn to fear the Lord your God**, as long as you live on the land which you are about to cross the Jordan to possess

Christ and belief are for everyone. All of Israel included the gentile, the alien, and the their children.

Matthew 16:12 Then they understood that He did not say to beware of the <u>leaven of bread, but of</u> **the teaching of the Pharisees and Sadducees.**

Remember, it's the lawless ones who don't enter into the Kingdom of God, they're cut off from the rest of Israel. If you're cut off from Israel, you're not part of the Covenant that God makes with the house of Israel.

Exodus 12:16-18 On the first day you shall have a holy assembly, and another holy assembly on the seventh day; no work at all shall be done on them, except what must be eaten by every person, that alone may be prepared by you. 17 You shall also observe the Feast of Unleavened Bread, for on this very day I brought your hosts out of the land of Egypt; therefore you shall observe this day throughout your generations as a permanent ordinance. 18 In the first month, on the fourteenth day of the month at evening, you shall eat unleavened bread, until the twenty-first day of the month at evening.

Passover and Unleavened Bread go hand-in-hand:

Matthew 26:17-19 Now on the first day of **Unleavened Bread** the disciples came to Jesus and asked, "Where do You want us to prepare for You to eat **the Passover?**" 18 And He said, "Go into the city to a certain man, and say to him, 'The Teacher says, "**My time is near; I am to keep the Passover at your house with My disciples.**"'" 19 The disciples did as Jesus had directed them; and they prepared the Passover.

God is serious about sin.

Exodus 12:19-20 Seven days there shall be no leaven found in your houses; for whoever eats what is leavened, that person shall be cut off from the congregation of Israel, **whether he is an alien or a native of the land**. 20 You shall not eat anything leavened; in all your dwellings you shall eat unleavened bread.'"

What is this parallel? Could it be exactly what we see heaven like?

> Revelation 21:5-8 And He who sits on the throne said, "Behold, I am making all things new." And He *said, "Write, for these words are faithful and true." 6 Then He said to me, "It is done. I am the Alpha and the Omega, **the beginning and the end**. I will give to the one who thirsts from the spring of the water of life without cost. 7 **He who overcomes will inherit these things, and I will be his God and he will be My son.** 8 But for the cowardly and unbelieving and abominable and murderers and immoral persons and sorcerers and idolaters and all liars, their part will be in the lake that burns with fire and brimstone, which is the second death."

Partaking of the leaven leads to separation from God.

> Luke 12:1 Under these circumstances, after so many thousands of people had gathered together that they were stepping on one another, He began saying to His disciples first of all, **"Beware of the leaven of the Pharisees, which is hypocrisy.**

We eat the Passover in haste because we are to flee from sin and run to God.

> Exodus 12:21-22 Then Moses called for all the elders of Israel and said to them, "Go and take for yourselves lambs according to your families, and slay the Passover lamb. 22 **You shall take a bunch of hyssop** and dip it in the blood which is in the basin, and apply some of the blood that is in the basin to the lintel and the two doorposts; and none of you shall go outside the door of his house until morning.

Again, in the parallel of blood and hyssop, we see the blood of Christ at the crucifixion and the hyssop branch in which they presented to Him.

> John 19: 29-30 A jar full of sour wine was standing there; so they put a sponge full of the sour wine <u>upon a branch of hyssop and brought it up to His mouth</u>. 30 Therefore when Jesus had received the sour wine, He said, "It is finished!" And He bowed His head and gave up His spirit.

> Exodus 12:23 For the Lord will pass through to smite the Egyptians; and **when He sees the blood on the lintel and on the two doorposts, the Lord will pass over the door and will not allow the destroyer to come into your houses to smite you**.

That's the whole crux of everything isn't it? He saves those who are in and destroys those who are without. Just like the ark and Noah, a preacher of righteousness. God saves those who are in and destroys those who are out. And everyone gets to choose where they are.

> John 10:7 So Jesus said to them again, "Truly, truly, I say to you, **I am the door of the sheep.** 8 <u>All who came before Me are thieves and robbers</u>, but <u>the sheep did not hear them.</u> 9 **I am the door; if anyone enters through Me, he will be saved, and will go in and out and find pasture.** 10 The thief comes only to steal and kill and destroy**; I came that they may have life, and have it abundantly.**

Others are thieves who steal, kill, and destroy. Men of violence. Just like in Genesis 6. Just as in the days of Noah.

Exodus 12:24-27 And **you shall observe this event as an ordinance for you and your children forever.** 25 When you enter the land which the Lord will give you, as He has promised, you shall observe this rite. 26 And when your children say to you, <u>'What does this rite mean to you?'</u> 27 you shall say, **<u>'It is a Passover sacrifice to the Lord who passed over the houses of the sons of Israel in Egypt when He smote the Egyptians, but spared our homes.'"</u>** And the people bowed low and worshiped.

When we do this now, we remind them that we were slaves to sin, just like we were slaves in Egypt. Christ who saved us from sin delivers us from death just like when He told us that when we put the blood of the lamb over the places where we live, He will spare us.

Luke 22:15 And He said to them, <u>"I have earnestly desired to eat this Passover with you before I suffer;</u> 16 for I say to you, I shall never again eat it until <u>it is fulfilled in the kingdom of God."</u> 17 And when He had taken a cup and given thanks, He said, "Take this and share it among yourselves; 18 for I say to you, I will not drink of the fruit of the vine from now on until the kingdom of God comes." 19 And when He had taken some bread and given thanks, He broke it and gave it to them, saying, **<u>"This is My body which is given for you; do this in remembrance of Me."</u>** 20 And in the same way He took the cup after they had eaten, saying, **<u>"This cup which is poured out for you is the new covenant in My blood.</u>**

Looking further in Exodus 12, we continue to see Christ in the Passover.

Exodus 12: 46 It is to be eaten in a single house; you are not to bring forth any of the flesh outside of the house**, nor are you to break any bone of it.**

John 19: 31 Then the Jews, because it was the day of preparation, so that the bodies would not remain on the cross on the Sabbath for that Sabbath was a high day)<u>, asked Pilate that their legs might be broken,</u> and that they might be taken away. 32 <u>So the soldiers came, and broke the legs of the first man and of the other who was crucified with Him;</u> 33 **but coming to Jesus, when they saw that He was already dead, they did not break His legs.**

The Passover is a beautiful, powerful picture of the redemption of humanity by Christ who walked in perfect submission to God's dominion. His example was showing us what we as the bride are to be

Luke 22:42-44 saying, "Father, **if <u>You are willing</u>**, remove this cup from Me; **yet not My will, <u>but Yours be done.</u>**" 43 Now an angel from heaven appeared to Him, strengthening Him. 44 **And being in agony He was praying very fervently**; and His sweat became like drops of blood, falling down upon the ground.

Knowing that He was going to go be beaten, flogged, slandered, spit on, abandoned, stabbed, and have to endure his beard being ripped out, generally some of the worst hardship that any person can ever endure ever, Christ—our example of headship and authority, our perfect example of how to be human, our flawless Bridegroom—looked to the Father and said "I'd like to not do this, but, I *will* serve You. I *will* walk

231

in *Your* dominion. *You* be lifted high and exalted." As men, we have a calling to show our brides that level of commitment to God as we live and die for them. Brides are called to show that kind of submission to God, so that the husband may also remember his calling. Not us, Him. My heart breaks every time I think of the suffering of Christ. The crowd of people who He loves. The splinters on the cross digging into his skin, the flies that He could not shoo from His face. It should have been us. We can strive to love Him better than we do ourselves. Did you know that unleavened bread is called the bread of affliction by God?

> Deuteronomy 16:3 You shall not eat leavened bread with it; seven days you shall eat with it unleavened bread, **the bread of affliction** (for you came out of the land of Egypt in haste), so that you may remember all the days of your life the day when you came out of the land of Egypt.

What does the Passover observance have to do with submission to God's dominion? He, as our Bridegroom, paid the price for our rebellion and our walking in self-determined dominance. He literally died to self as our example. He taught us how to sacrifice our will for God's will. He redeemed us with His blood that we might cease our defiance. Have you considered the resurrection that occurred after the Passover? Did you know that is a significant appointed time to offer the first fruits of the harvest to God?

Leviticus 23:9- 15 Then the Lord spoke to Moses, saying, 10 "Speak to the sons of Israel and say to them, 'When you enter the land which I am going to give to you and reap its harvest, **then you shall bring in the sheaf of the first fruits of your harvest to the priest.** 11 He shall wave the sheaf before the Lord for you to be accepted; on the day after the sabbath the priest shall wave it. 12 Now on the day when you wave the sheaf, you shall offer a male lamb one year old without defect for a burnt offering to the Lord. 13 Its grain offering shall then be two-tenths of an ephah of fine flour mixed with oil, an offering by fire to the Lord for a soothing aroma, with its drink offering, a fourth of a hin of wine. 14 **Until this same day, until you have brought in the offering of your God,** you shall eat neither bread nor roasted grain nor new growth. It is to be a perpetual statute throughout your generations in all your dwelling places.

1 Corinthians 15:20-22 **But now Christ has been raised from the dead, the first fruits of those who are asleep.** 21 For since by a man came death, by a man also came the resurrection of the dead. 22 For as in Adam all die, so also in Christ all will be made alive.

Looking further at the contrast of the wheat:

Luke 3:17 His winnowing fork is in His hand to thoroughly clear His threshing floor, and to gather the wheat into His barn; but He will burn up the chaff with unquenchable fire."

Matthew 13:24–30 Jesus presented another parable to them, saying, "The kingdom of heaven may be compared to a man who sowed good seed in his field. 25 But while his men were sleeping, his enemy came and sowed tares among the wheat, and went away. 26 But when the wheat sprouted and bore grain, then the tares became evident also. 27 The slaves of the landowner came and said to him, 'Sir, did you not sow good seed in your field? How then does it have tares?' 28 And he said to them, 'An enemy has done this!' The slaves *said to him, 'Do you want us, then, to go and gather them up?' 29 But he *said, 'No; for while you are gathering up the tares, you may uproot the wheat with them. 30 **Allow both to grow together until the harvest**; and in **the time of the harvest I will say to the reapers, "First gather up the tares and bind them in bundles to burn them up; but gather the wheat into my barn."**

36 Then He left the crowds and went into the house. And His disciples came to Him and said, "Explain to us the parable of the tares of the field." 37 And He said, "The one who sows the good seed is the Son of Man, 38 and the field is the world; and as for the good seed, these are the sons of the kingdom; and the tares are the sons of the evil one; 39 and the enemy who sowed them is the devil, and the harvest is the end of the age; and the reapers are angels. 40 So just as the tares are gathered up and burned with fire, so shall it be at the end of the age. 41 The Son of Man will send forth His angels, and **they will gather out of His kingdom all stumbling blocks**, and **those who commit lawlessness**, 42 and will **throw them into the furnace of fire**; in that place there will be weeping and gnashing of teeth. 43 **Then the righteous will shine forth as the sun in the kingdom of their Father. He who has ears, let him hear.**

We know that the wheat symbolizes the harvest of souls. Do you know how to tell the difference between the wheat and the tares? At the time of the harvest, the wheat, when ripe with grain, bows down. The tares stand upright and proudly defiant. Tares are poisonous just like Jude speaks of those who are in the church but are "hidden reefs in the love feasts", doomed for destruction. They may have the appearance of wheat but they will be gathered together and thrown in the fire instead of harvested with those that produced "fruit" who are gathered to the storehouse of God.

Just like in Genesis, we see this threefold classification of people, those who are actively against God, those who are actively for God, and those who are neither. The tares, the wheat and the chaff. In Revelation 3 it states, "I wish you were either hot or cold, but because you were lukewarm, I will vomit you out of my mouth." Those who are walking in the dominion of God, those who are walking in the dominance of flesh, and those who have one foot in the world and one foot in the Church. Perhaps that is a reason that God has said that we are not to plant two types of seed in the same field—because we are not to be mixing the things of God with the things of the world. Friendship with the world is hostility towards God.

> Leviticus 23:15-21 'You shall also count for yourselves from the day after the sabbath, from the day when you brought in the sheaf of the wave offering; there shall be seven complete sabbaths. 16 You shall count fifty days to the day after the seventh sabbath; then you shall present a new grain offering to the Lord. 17 You shall bring in from your dwelling places two loaves of bread for a wave offering, made of two-tenths of an

ephah; they shall be of a fine flour, baked with leaven as first fruits to the Lord. 18 Along with the bread you shall present seven one year old male lambs without defect, and a bull of the herd and two rams; they are to be a burnt offering to the Lord, with their grain offering and their drink offerings, an offering by fire of a soothing aroma to the Lord. 19 You shall also offer one male goat for a sin offering and two male lambs one year old for a sacrifice of peace offerings. 20 The priest shall then wave them with the bread of the first fruits for a wave offering with two lambs before the Lord; they are to be holy to the Lord for the priest. 21 On this same day you shall make a proclamation as well; you are to have a holy convocation. **You shall do no laborious work.** It is to be a perpetual statute in all your dwelling places throughout your generations.

The time between the Passover and Pentecost is called the counting of the Omer. This is the 50 days previously mentioned. When you see that there were three days and three nights in the grave, and then seven days after that He appeared to Thomas, then for 40 days He was teaching all the things concerning Him, we incredibly arrive at 50 days.

John 20:24-2924 But Thomas, one of the twelve, called Didymus, was not with them when Jesus came. 25 So the other disciples were saying to him, "We have seen the Lord!" But he said to them, "Unless I see in His hands the imprint of the nails, and put my finger into the place of the nails, and put my hand into His side, I will not believe." 26 After eight days His disciples were again inside, and Thomas with them. Jesus *came, the doors having been shut, and stood in their midst and said, "Peace be with you." 27 Then He *said to Thomas, "Reach here with your finger, and see My hands; and reach here your hand and put it into My side; and do not be unbelieving, but believing." 28 Thomas answered and said to Him, "My Lord and my God!" 29 Jesus *said to him, "Because you have seen Me, have you believed? Blessed are they who did not see, and yet believed."

Acts 1:2-3 To these He also presented Himself alive after His suffering, by many convincing proofs, appearing to them over a period of forty days and speaking of the things concerning the kingdom of God. 4 Gathering them together, He commanded them not to leave Jerusalem, but to wait for what the Father had promised, "Which," He said, "you heard of from Me.

The Passover from Egypt to the outpouring of the Spirit at Shavuot is the same as the Passover of Christ's sacrifice and then the outpouring of the Spirit at Pentecost. Christ commissioned the church to walk not in the flesh but by the power of His Holy Spirit.

Leviticus 23:23 Again the Lord spoke to Moses, saying, 24 "Speak to the sons of Israel, saying, 'In the seventh month on the first of the month you shall have a rest, a reminder by blowing of trumpets, a holy convocation. 25 You shall not do any laborious work, but you shall present an offering by fire to the Lord.'"

Here we have God establishing the day where there is the blasting of the trumpets or shofars as a Holy convocation. What might that teach us about God? What might this decree be a picture of in the New Testament?

> 1 Thessalonians 4:16 For the Lord Himself will descend from heaven with a shout, with the voice of the archangel <u>and with the trumpet of God</u>, and the dead in Christ will rise first.

> 1 Corinthians 15:52 in a moment, in the twinkling of an eye,<u> at the last trumpet; for the trumpet will sound</u>, and the dead will be raised imperishable, and we will be changed.

Christ is returning as trumpets are the proclamation of the King of Israel. Let's look at The Day of Atonement:

> Leviticus 23:26 The Lord spoke to Moses, saying, 27 "On exactly the tenth day of this seventh month is the day of atonement; it shall be a holy convocation for you, and you shall humble your souls and present an offering by fire to the Lord. 28 **You shall not do any work** on this same day, for it is a day of atonement, to make atonement on your behalf before the Lord your God. 29 If there is any person who will not humble himself on this same day, he shall be cut off from his people. 30 **As for any person who does any work on this same day, that person I will destroy from among his people. 31 You shall do no work at all.** <u>It is to be a perpetual statute throughout your generations in all your dwelling places.</u> 32 **It is to be a sabbath of complete rest to you,** and

you shall humble your souls; on the ninth of the month at evening, from evening until evening you shall keep your sabbath.

What does this teach us about Christ? That *we* are not the ones who atone for ourselves. Over and over and over again, this passage states that at the Atonement, we do not work. It is *only* in the work of our Messiah and Savior Christ that we are atoned for. There are countless Scriptures that show that we are not saved by our works. We may be sanctified by doing the works of God *after* He has saved us, but that is by no means contributing anything to our salvation which rests on the work of Christ alone. He did what we could never do for ourselves.

Ephesians 2:8-9 For <u>by grace you have been saved through faith</u>; **and that not of yourselves,** it is **the gift of God;** 9 **not as a result of works,** so that **no one may boast.**

1 John 2:2 and **He Himself is the propitiation for our sins**; and not for ours only, but also for those of the whole world.

Hebrews 9:12-14 and not through the blood of goats and calves, <u>but through His own blood,</u> He entered the holy place once for all, having obtained eternal redemption. 13 For if the blood of goats and bulls and the ashes of a heifer sprinkling those who have been defiled sanctify for the cleansing of the flesh, 14 how much more will the blood of Christ, who through the eternal Spirit <u>offered Himself without blemish to God, cleanse your conscience from dead works to serve the living God?</u>

There is much to be said about Christ as High priest, going into the Holy of Holies as the High Priest. A High Priest who is without sin who therefore doesn't have to offer the sin offering for the priests like the Levitical priests were instructed to do, because He Himself is without sin. If I wrote everything there is to say on this parallel, it would be an entire, separate book. This brings us to the feast of Booths/Sukkot/Tabernacles, also called the Marriage Supper of the Lamb.

> Leviticus 23:33-44 Again the Lord spoke to Moses, saying, 34 "Speak to the sons of Israel, saying, 'On the fifteenth of this seventh month is **the Feast of Booths** for <u>seven days to the Lord</u>. 35 On the first day is a holy convocation; **you shall do no laborious work of any kind**. 36 For seven days you shall present an offering by fire to the Lord. On the eighth day you shall have a holy convocation and present an offering by fire to the Lord; it is an assembly. **You shall do no laborious work**. 37 'These are the appointed times of the Lord which you shall proclaim as holy convocations, to present offerings by fire to the Lord—burnt offerings and grain offerings, sacrifices and drink offerings, each day's matter on its own day— 38 <u>besides those of the sabbaths of the Lord</u>, and besides your gifts and besides all your votive and freewill offerings, which you give to the Lord. 39 'On exactly the fifteenth day of the seventh month, when you have gathered in the crops of the land, <u>you shall celebrate the feast of the Lord for seven days, with a rest on the first day and a rest on the eighth day</u>. 40 Now on the first day you shall take for yourselves the foliage of beautiful trees, <u>palm branches</u> and boughs of leafy trees and willows of

the brook, **and you shall rejoice before the Lord your God for seven days**. 41 You shall thus celebrate it as a feast to the Lord for seven days in the year. It shall be a perpetual statute throughout your generations; you shall celebrate it in the seventh month. 42 You shall live in booths for seven days; all the native-born in Israel shall live in booths, 43 so that your generations may know that I had the sons of Israel live in booths when I brought them out from the land of Egypt. I am the Lord your God.'" 44 So Moses declared to the sons of Israel the appointed times of the Lord.

What parallels do we see from God's commands here and what do they teach us about Christ?

Revelation 7:9 After these things I looked, and behold, a great multitude which no one could count, from every nation and all tribes and peoples and tongues, standing before the throne and before the Lamb, clothed in white robes, **and palm branches were in their hands.**

One of the first things we see is that Egypt represents sin and bondage and slavery, and God redeemed us from those things. He draws us out and causes us to dwell with Him.

Galatians 5:1 It was for freedom that Christ set us free; therefore keep standing firm and do not be subject again to a yoke of slavery.

Romans 7:14 For we know that the Law is spiritual, but I am of flesh, sold into <u>bondage to sin.</u>

John 8:34-36 Jesus answered them, "Truly, truly, I say to you, <u>everyone who commits sin is the slave of sin.</u> 35 The slave does not remain in the house forever; the son does remain forever. 36 <u>So if the Son makes you free, you will be free indeed.</u>

We are freed from sin, drawn out of Egypt, and God dwells among us. This is also what we see in Revelation when heaven comes down:

Revelation 21:10-14 And he carried me away in the Spirit to a great and high mountain, <u>and showed me the holy city, Jerusalem, coming down out of heaven from God,</u> 11 having the glory of God. Her brilliance was like a very costly stone, as a stone of crystal-clear jasper. 12 It had a great and high wall, with twelve gates, and at the gates twelve angels; and names were written on them, which are the names of the twelve tribes of the sons of Israel. 13 There were three gates on the east and three gates on the north and three gates on the south and three gates on the west. 14 And the wall of the city had twelve foundation stones, and on them were the twelve names of the twelve apostles of the Lamb.

We see that this Holy city comes down and only the redeemed people can enter into it.

Revelation 21:23 And the city has no need of the sun or of the moon to shine on it, for the glory of God has illumined it, and its lamp is the Lamb. 24 The nations will walk by its light, and the kings of the earth will bring their glory into it. 25 In the daytime (for there will be no night there) its gates will never be closed; 26 and they will bring the glory and the honor of the nations into it; 27 <u>and nothing unclean, and no one who practices abomination and lying, shall ever come into it, but only those whose names are written in the Lamb's book of life.</u>

We don't enter into the Most Holy Place where God dwells by imposing our own dominance and ways. We can see this at the second coming of Christ in Zechariah 14:

Zacheriah 14:16-21 Then it will come about that <u>any who are left of all the nations</u> that went against Jerusalem will go up from year to yea<u>r to worship the King, the Lord of hosts, and to celebrate the Feast of Booths</u>. 17 And it will be that <u>whichever of the families of the earth does not go up</u> to Jerusalem to worship the King, the Lord of hosts, there will be no rain on them. 18 If the family of Egypt does not go up **or enter**, then no rain will fall on them; **it will be the plague with which the Lord smites the nations who do not go up to celebrate the Feast of Booths**. 19 This will be the punishment of Egypt, <u>and the punishment of all the nations</u> **who do not** <u>go up to celebrate the Feast of Booths.</u> 20 In that day there will be inscribed on the bells of the horses, "HOLY TO THE LORD." And the cooking pots in the Lord's house will be like the bowls before the altar. 21 Every cooking pot in Jerusalem and in Judah will be holy to the Lord of hosts; <u>and all who sacrifice will come and take of them and boil in them.</u>

And there will no longer be a Canaanite in the house of the Lord of hosts in that day.

Note that it is disobedience to not come up to the feast. That passage in Zechariah 14 begins with the Savior splitting the temple mount, as prophesied. There are a lot of deep prophetic parallels that warrant attention and study, but I'd like to look more at the aspects of this feast and the marriage feast of the Lamb.

Did you know that the first recorded miracle of Christ was at the wedding where He turned water into wine?

> John 2:2-11 On the third day there was a wedding in Cana of Galilee, and the mother of Jesus was there; 2 and both Jesus and His disciples were invited to the wedding. 3 When the wine ran out, the mother of Jesus *said to Him, "They have no wine." 4 And Jesus *said to her, <u>"Woman, what does that have to do with us? My hour has not yet come."</u> 5 His mother *said to the servants, "Whatever He says to you, do it." 6 <u>Now there were six stone waterpots set there for the Jewish custom of purification</u>, containing twenty or thirty gallons each. 7 Jesus *said to them, "Fill the waterpots with water." So they filled them up to the brim. 8 And He *said to them, "Draw some out now and take it to the headwaiter." So they took it to him. 9 When the headwaiter tasted the water which had become wine, and did not know where it came from (but the servants who had drawn the water knew), the headwaiter *called the bridegroom, <u>10 and *said to him, "Every man serves the good wine first, and when the people have drunk freely, then he</u>

serves the poorer wine; but you have kept the good wine until now." 11 This beginning of His signs Jesus did in Cana of Galilee, and manifested His glory, and His disciples believed in Him.

Is there perhaps significance to this as He says, "My hour has not yet come"? Granted, Christ said this many places regarding the miracles and the concern that He would be killed before His time. Could He have been referencing the Marriage Supper of the Lamb? When we look at the parallels of this wedding miracle and the passage regarding this feast in Deuteronomy, we see these parallels:

Deuteronomy 14:22 "You shall surely tithe all the produce from what you sow, which comes out of the field every year. 23 **You shall eat in the presence of the Lord your God**, at the place where He chooses to establish His name, the tithe of your grain, your new wine, your oil, and the firstborn of your herd and your flock, so that you may learn to fear the Lord your God always. 24 If the distance is so great for you that you are not able to bring the tithe, since the place where the Lord your God chooses to set His name is too far away from you when the Lord your God blesses you, 25 then you shall exchange it for money, and bind the money in your hand and go to the place which the Lord your God chooses. 26 You may spend the money for whatever your heart desires: for oxen, or sheep, **or wine, or strong drink**, or whatever your heart desires; and there you shall eat **in the presence of the Lord your God** and **rejoice**, you and your household.

Both passages are about a wedding, both passages are regarding the good wine and the heart's desires. Christ says that He desires to drink the wine but will not drink again until He comes again at *this* marriage feast:

> Matthew 26:29 But I say to you, I will not drink of this fruit of the vine **from now on until that day** <u>when I drink it new with you in My Father's kingdom.</u>"

Do you see the parallel of the vessels of purification which represent us, being filled with water, which parallels the living water, and through God's purification, our lives become as that sweet wine. It is only those who are purified who will enter into the dwelling place that comes down from Heaven. It is only those who wash their robes who are part of this marriage supper at the end of the harvest

> Revelation 22:14 Blessed are those who wash their robes, <u>so that they may have the right to the tree of life</u>, and <u>may enter by the gates into the city</u>.

There is an entire parable about this response:

> Matthew 22:1-14 Jesus spoke to them again in parables, saying, 2 <u>"The kingdom of heaven may be compared to a king who gave a wedding feast</u> for his son. 3 And he sent out his slaves <u>to call those who had been invited</u> to the wedding feast, and they were unwilling to come. 4 Again he sent out other slaves saying, 'Tell those who have been invited, "Behold, I have prepared my dinner; my oxen and my fattened livestock are all butchered and everything is ready; come to the wedding

feast.'" **5 But they paid no attention and went their way, one to his own farm, another to his business**, 6 and the rest seized his slaves and mistreated them and killed them. 7 But the king was enraged, <u>and he sent his armies and destroyed those murderers and set their city on fire.</u> 8 Then he *said to his slaves, 'The wedding is ready, but those who were invited were not worthy. 9 Go therefore to the main highways, and as many as you find there, invite to the wedding feast.' 10 Those slaves went out into the streets and gathered together all they found, both evil and good; <u>and the wedding hall was filled with dinner guests.</u>11 "But when the king came in to look over the dinner guests, **he saw a man there who was not dressed in wedding clothes**, 12 and he *said to him, 'Friend, **how did you come in here without wedding clothes**?' And the man was speechless. 13 Then the king said to the servants, '<u>Bind him hand and foot, and throw him into the outer darkness;</u> in that place there will be weeping and gnashing of teeth.' 14 For many are called, but few are chosen."

Just like the tares among the wheat, just like those who come to Him saying, "didn't we cast out demons and prophecy in your name?" whom He says, "Depart from me you workers of lawlessness, I never knew you". Self-determination got us exiled from the garden, and all of history has been God patiently giving us examples and teaching us how to not get kicked out of the garden when we're restored. As we rid ourselves of our trying to "be like God, determining good and evil", we turn back to submission to the Bridegroom, that we may be at peace. We wash our robes so that we can attend that wedding. We can be that good wine. We are the new Covenant believers.

Jeremiah 3131 "Behold, days are coming," declares the Lord, "when I will make a new covenant with the house of Israel and with the house of Judah, 32 not like the covenant which I made with their fathers in the day I took them by the hand to bring them out of the land of Egypt, **My covenant which they broke**, although **I was a husband to them**," declares the Lord. 33 "But this is the covenant which I will make with the house of Israel after those days," declares the Lord, **"I will put My law within them and on their heart I will write it**; and I will be their God, and they shall be My people. 34 **They will not teach again, each man his neighbor and each man his brother, saying, 'Know the Lord,' for they will all know Me, from the least of them to the greatest of them,"** declares the Lord, "for I will forgive their iniquity, and their sin I will remember no more."

35 Thus says the Lord, Who gives the sun for light by day And the fixed order of the moon and the stars for light by night, Who stirs up the sea so that its waves roar; The Lord of hosts is His name: 36 "If this fixed order departs From before Me," declares the Lord, "Then the offspring of Israel also will cease From being a nation before Me forever." 37 Thus says the Lord, "If the heavens above can be measured And the foundations of the earth searched out below, Then I will also cast off all the offspring of Israel For all that they have done," declares the Lord.

38 **"Behold, days are coming,"** declares the Lord, "when the city will be rebuilt for the Lord from the Tower of Hananel to

the Corner Gate. 39 The measuring line will go out farther straight ahead to the hill Gareb; then it will turn to Goah. 40 And the whole valley of the dead bodies and of the ashes, and all the fields as far as the brook Kidron, <u>to the corner of the Horse Gate toward the east, shall be holy to the Lord</u>; it **will not** be plucked up or overthrown anymore forever."

We already read about that horse gate in Zechariah 14:

Zecheriah 14:20 <u>In that day there will be inscribed on the bells of the horses, "HOLY TO THE LORD."</u> And the cooking pots in the Lord's house will be like the bowls before the altar.

The difference between the covenants is that we're not going to break the new one! We've washed our robes, we'll be given new bodies. We've forsaken the rebellion and the ways of dominance over others and against God. We've put the fruit back on the tree and are restored by His work, and we will live before the King of Glory by His work and love the Bridegroom forever!

Job 25:2-4 <u>"Dominion and awe belong to Him Who establishes peace **in His heights**.</u>
3 "Is there any number to His troops?
And upon whom does His light not rise?
4 "How then can a man be just with God?
Or how can he be clean who is born of woman?

Philippians 4:11-13 11 <u>Not that I speak from want</u>, for I have learned to be content in whatever circumstances I am. 12 I know how to get along with humble means, and I also know how to live in prosperity; <u>in any and every circumstance I have learned the secret of being filled and going hungry, both of having abundance and suffering need.</u> 13 I can do **all things through Him** who strengthens me.

Way back at the beginning of this book, I discussed how the church has strayed and splintered and housed wolves from the pulpits that desire self-adulation. We discussed how the congregations have shifted from healthy bodies to places of strange fire, leading to disorder, chaos, and madness. That is the fruit that we have eaten that has expelled us from the garden. Where we once only knew God's goodness, we now know with intimate awareness that which is evil. The world will continue to get stranger and darker as long as we insist on standing on our own intellectual hubris and flesh-based self-reliance. Every day is an opportunity to walk in the ways of God, to surrender to His Spirit. Every day is an opportunity for men to break the generational patterns of destruction that walk in flesh and emotional stonewalling that leads to self-devaluation. Every day is a chance for women to walk in the grace and forgiveness of the bride who reminds and inspires men to rise to the created standard that God has called them to. Every day is a chance to bridge the gaps between men and women, God and man, and repair the damage that we do to one another when we walk in dominance. Every day is a chance to let God show us He is in control, that His way is better, that His plan is the best.

If we as a church, as a body of believers, are looking to repair that which has been lost in a broken world and put to rest the hostility that lives between men and women, we must learn from the mistakes that separate us. We must learn what makes men seek out dominance over their fellow men and seek to dominate over women, before they grow to be the men who become monsters. We must see the patterns of broken women who seek the power and dominance and self-exaltation from both the pulpit and the household. We must understand that to repair a fallen world that is rotten with our own selfishness and our wrestling control away from the fingers of God, we must do as God Himself orders:

> Luke 9:23 And He was saying to them all, "If <u>anyone </u>wishes to come after Me, he **must** deny himself, and <u>take up his cross daily</u> and follow Me.

God is a God of order, and that order is Him first.
The example of how to be a good husband is to submit to God first.
The example of how to be the bride of Christ is to submit to God first.
The example of how to be a righteous nation is to put God first.
The example of how to lead a righteous church is to put Him first.
The way to meet the needs of a dying world full of darkness is to put God first.
We can only stop propagating destruction by returning to submission to Him first.
The best way to bring healing is to come to Him first.
The only way we can love ourselves and our neighbor the way that we are supposed to is to put Him first in all matters, big or small, every joy or heartbreak, laughter or fear...

We shall have no other gods before Him.

BONUS CHAPTER

Questions for Pastors

Through my years of studying the Law of God and having probably thousands of online discussions over the applicability of God's Law, I kept running into people who were at the time saying, "that's not what my pastor says". Inspired by a meme I saw from 119 Ministries asking 10 questions about the millennial reign of Christ, in time, I began collecting "questions for pastors". Here for your enjoyment are those many, many questions that you can ask a pastor in hopes of developing a full consistency with God and His Word.

If we are to worship God in Spirit and in truth, and Psalm 119:151 says God's commands/Law are truth, and Ezekiel 36:26-27 says the Spirit causes us to follow the Law, why do we assume that the Spirit is opposed to God's Law? Did the truth somehow become not the truth?

Why did God have to tell Noah to not eat the animals but instead eat what the animals eat in Genesis 6:20-21 if they didn't eat animals before the flood?

How did Cain and Abel know what and when to sacrifice, and God rejected Cain's offering?

If we are not to follow the Law of God, why do you collect tithes that were supposed to go to the Levites? If a mixed multitude came out of Egypt, and a mixed multitude was at Sinai, why do we say that that covenant was only for the Jews? If the Law of God was only for the Jews, why does God say over and over that the same Law was for Gentiles too?

If the Holy Spirit wasn't given until Acts, why is it there in Genesis 1:2?

If Jesus says that the greatest commands are to love God and love your neighbor, and he was quoting Deuteronomy 6:4-9 and Leviticus 19:18, is Jesus telling us to obey God's Law?

Why does Joshua 8:33 call the gentile part of Israel if gentiles aren't Israel?

If Paul agrees with everything in the Law and the Prophets and still practices Christ-centered Judaism as stated in Acts 24:14, why is Christianity not still considered a sect of Judaism?

In Psalm 1:1-2, we see that the Law is contrary to the council of the wicked. Shouldn't we follow it?

If Jesus broke the 4th command, then he wouldn't be sinless, correct? If Jesus didn't break the Sabbath, shouldn't we also keep the Sabbath like Him?

If in Matthew 5 Jesus says that teaching people not to follow the commands of God/Law of God makes you the least in heaven, why are we not teaching people to follow the commands of God/Law of God?

If all Scripture is given by inspiration of God, and is profitable for doctrine, for reproof, for correction, for instruction in righteousness, why do we say that Leviticus 11 is not?

Deuteronomy 8 says, "You shall remember all the way which the Lord your God has led you in the wilderness these forty years, that He might humble you, testing you, to know what was in your heart, whether you would keep His commandments or not." Since God doesn't change, is it safe to say He still tests hearts to see if we will obey His commands?

Deuteronomy 8 says, "Thus you are to know in your heart that the Lord your God was disciplining you just as a man disciplines his son. Therefore, you shall keep the commandments of the Lord your God, to walk in His ways and to fear Him." Doesn't obeying the commands of God go with Proverbs 12:1 where it says, "Whoever loves discipline loves knowledge, But he who hates reproof is stupid."

Deuteronomy 7 says, "Know therefore that the Lord your God, He is God, the faithful God, who keeps His covenant and His lovingkindness to a thousandth generation with those who love Him and keep His commandments; but repays those who hate Him to their faces, to destroy them; He will not delay with him who hates Him, He will repay him to his face." Can it be said that a hatred for God's commandments is hatred for God also?

Deuteronomy 6 says, "So the Lord commanded us to observe all these statutes, to fear the Lord our God for our good always and for our survival, as it is today. It will be righteousness for us if we are careful to observe all this commandment before the Lord our God, just as He commanded us." Isn't choosing God's righteousness by obedience the same as living as Christ?

Jude says, "In the last time there will be mockers, following after their own ungodly lusts." These are the ones who cause divisions, worldly-minded, devoid of the Spirit. If the Spirit writes the Law of God on the hearts of New Covenant believers, then isn't Jude warning against any who would mock those keeping God's Laws?

Malachi 2:2-3 speaks of God's anger for people holding feasts and festivities that do not honor Him. We know that Christmas and Easter are not in the Bible; is it possible that God could be talking about these customs that have commonly replaced God's Holy days?

If in the end times the Law will go forth from Zion as it says in Isaiah 2:2-3, why do pastors say that it was "nailed to the cross" and not to be observed?

If Proverbs says, "The fear of the Lord is the beginning of knowledge; Fools despise wisdom and instruction," does that mean that those who reject the Law/Instructions of God are fools?

In Mark 7, we see the religious leaders rebuked for holding to their interpretations over what the Scriptures say. How would you react if a congregant pointed out that in Leviticus 11, our unchanging God states that specific animals are not, nor ever were, for food?

Jeremiah 23 says, "The anger of the Lord will not turn back Until He has performed and carried out the purposes of His heart; In the last days you will clearly understand it. I did not send these prophets, But they ran. I did not speak to them, But they prophesied. But if they had stood in My council, Then they would have announced My words to My people, And would have turned them back from their evil way and from the evil of their deeds." If we are in the last days as most agree, shouldn't the priests and prophets be proclaiming a return to God's Law/His ways/His deeds?

God says in Jeremiah 11, "Cursed is the man who does not heed the words of this covenant which I commanded your forefathers in the day that I brought them out of the land of Egypt, from the iron furnace, saying, 'Listen to My voice, and do according to all which I command you; so you shall be My people, and I will be your God." Shouldn't we heed the words of God's covenant, seeing as how the New Covenant is the same, except we don't break it?

In the book of Jeremiah, God is greatly grieved and in anguish over people neglecting His ways and His commands, forgoing His Law for their own. We know God doesn't change, so why would He not feel the same way when we do the same things today?

Jeremiah 5 says, "For the house of Israel and the house of Judah Have dealt very treacherously with Me," declares the Lord. They have lied about the Lord And said, "Not He; Misfortune will not come on us, And we will not see sword or famine." Many today preach that there is no difference between Israel and Judah; shouldn't we be concerned when they also preach that we will not see sword or famine?

Isaiah 9:6 says, "For a child will be born to us, a son will be given to us; And the government will rest on His shoulders; And His name will be called Wonderful Counselor, Mighty God, Eternal Father, Prince of Peace." As we believe that Christ is God, then God's Law and Christ's Law would be the same Law, right?

Colossians 3 says, "Let the word of Christ richly dwell within you, with all wisdom teaching and admonishing one another with psalms and hymns and spiritual songs, singing with thankfulness in your hearts to God." Does that mean that we should use Psalms 119 for admonishing?

In church, we often hear that it's just Jews and Gentiles. Why does Christ say in Luke 22, "so that you may eat and drink at my table in my kingdom and sit on thrones, judging the *twelve* tribes of Israel." Doesn't that mean not just Judah?

Ezekiel 37 says, "This is what the Sovereign Lord says: I am going to take the stick of Joseph—which is in Ephraim's hand—and of the Israelite tribes associated with him, and join it to Judah's stick. I will make them into a single stick of wood, and they will become one in my hand." Why is it commonly taught that Judah (Jews) are the only ones that are Israel?

We are called to be "doers of the Word and not hearers only," as James 1:22-25 states. Doesn't that Word include all the Commands of God as 2 Timothy 3:16-17 points to?

If we interpret Paul as saying it doesn't matter if you keep the Sabbath in Colossians 2:16, How can Hebrews 4:9-11 say not keeping the Sabbath as God does is disobedience?

We are New Covenant believers. If His Law is written on our hearts as Hebrews 10:16 states, why don't we have a desire to keep it?

In Psalms 19:10, it says that the commands of God are greater than gold. Why do we often hear sermons about money but not enough about being obedient to the commands of God? Psalms 19:9 says, "The fear of the Lord is clean, enduring forever; The judgments of the Lord are true; they are righteous altogether." If God's Law is true and righteous altogether, why wouldn't we follow it?

Psalms 19:8 says, "The precepts of the Lord are right, rejoicing the heart; The commandment of the Lord is pure, enlightening the eyes." Why do many modern pastors preach the opposite of this in reference to the Law of God?

Deuteronomy 28:1-14 talks about the great blessings in following the commands of God. Why would Christ supposedly get rid of these blessings?

Exodus 15:26 says that the commands of God are healing. Why do we often interpret them as being bondage?

Deuteronomy 7:11-15 says that the Law and commands of God bring healing and blessings; why would that be interpreted as bondage?

Deuteronomy 7:12 refers to the Covenant as a Covenant of Love. Why do we characterize the Covenant as bondage and oppression?

Scripture shows that there would have been 14 giraffes on the Ark with Noah. Doesn't the fact that there is a classification of clean and unclean before Sinai poke holes in the idea of dispensationalism?

It is written that even the demons believe and tremble (James 2:19). So, wouldn't we be at the same level as the demons if all we did was believe?

Scripture says that God is true and every man is a liar. In Psalm 119:142, it states that God's Law is truth. If it became not truth, wouldn't that make God a liar?

In Isaiah 63:10-14, it states that they grieved the Holy Spirit. Why do we often hear that the New Covenant is new because it includes the Holy Spirit, when the original covenant clearly included the Holy Spirit?

Psalm 119:98 states that the commands of God/His Law makes one wiser than their enemies. Why would that be considered a burden?

The Sabbath was instituted before sin entered the world and before Adam had sinned. How can the law change something that predates sin or the need for the law?

Isaiah 5:24 says, "...For they have rejected the law of the Lord of Hosts and despised the word of the Holy One of Israel." Isn't a rejection of the Law of God the same thing as despising the Holy One of Israel?

Joshua 1:7-8 states that following the Law of God is great success. Why do we interpret that as a legalistic failure?

In Judges 2:22, Judges 3:1 and 4, we see that God tests His
people to see if they will obey His commands. Is there any
indicator that God has stopped doing this?
We know from Scripture that the golden calf was worshiping
God in pagan ways, and Judges 2:12-14 talks about forsaking
God and worshiping other gods in those ways. Are there
customs that the church has adapted that are not in line with
what God teaches as acceptable?

Doesn't Deuteronomy 5:29-33 and the New Covenant
outlined in Jeremiah 32:38-42 make the same points?

Why do we interpret it as only Jews leaving Egypt when
Scripture states that it was a mixed multitude in Exodus 12:38?

Mark 3:24-25 says a kingdom/house divided against itself
cannot stand. Wouldn't that mean that the Law of Christ and
God's Law can't be in opposition since the Word stands
forever?

If we are to interpret the Sabbath having been done away with
due to it being addressed in the Law of God, how do we
reconcile that it was given before Sinai as Genesis 2:1-3 shows?

John 14:10 says, "If you keep my commands, you will remain
in my love, just as I have kept my Father's commands and
remain in his love." Doesn't that support the notion that we
should be obeying the Law of God?

John 14:15 says, "If you love me, keep my commands." How do we physically do that?

Can it be possible for the Law of Christ and the Law of God to be different Laws, since Christ obeys God and is of God, teaching obedience to the instructions of God as He Himself follows?

Ephesians 6:4 reads, "Fathers, do not exasperate your children; instead, bring them up in the training and instruction of the Lord." Aren't the instructions of the Lord the commands of God, His Law?

Romans 3:20 states, "Therefore no one will be declared righteous in God's sight by the works of the law; rather, through the law we become conscious of our sin". How can we repent of sin, if we are not conscious of it? Doesn't that mean we should study the Law of God for repentance?

In Matthew 26, Christ says, "You know that after two days the Passover is coming, and the Son of Man is to be handed over for crucifixion." Why does the church recognize Easter instead of Passover?

If the Law was done away with, why does Ezekiel 40-48 detail the return of Levites, offerings, and a Temple?

How is it possible for Christ to be a righteous judge if Christ allegedly abolished the Law of God? By what standard would He judge?

Titus 2 says, "But as for you, speak the things which are fitting for sound doctrine. Older men are to be temperate, dignified, sensible, sound in faith, in love, in perseverance." Doesn't the perseverance of the believer outlined in Revelation 14:12 indicate that we are to keep the commands of God along with faith in Christ?

In Titus 1, Paul says, "They profess to know God, but by their deeds they deny Him, being detestable and disobedient and worthless for any good deed". Aren't the deeds that people should be doing the commands of God as Christ states in Matthew 7:21-23?

2 Peter 2 states that the way of Balaam is the love of wickedness, stumbling, and false prophecy, and Revelation 2 says that by eating unclean things and committing immorality, Christ makes war against them. Isn't the definition of wicked in Greek *athesmos*: one who breaks through the restraint of Law and gratifies his lusts, and Psalm 119:9-11 says that God's Law helps a man keep pure?

In Amos 2:4, God says, "For three sins of Judah, even for four, I will not relent. Because they have rejected the law of the Lord and have not kept his decrees, because they have been led astray by false gods, the gods their ancestors followed." If God hates it when people don't follow the Law of the Lord, which are His commands, and God doesn't change, why do we often hear that the Law is not to be followed?

1 Timothy 6:3-4 say "If anyone advocates a different doctrine and does not agree with sound words, those of our Lord Jesus Christ, and with the doctrine conforming to godliness, he is conceited and understands nothing; but he has a morbid interest in controversial questions and disputes about words..." Is there anything in the Law of God that isn't conforming to godliness, and doesn't Scripture say that the commands of God are sound doctrine?

In 1 Timothy 4, Paul writes, "paying attention to deceitful spirits and doctrines of demons, ... men who forbid marriage and advocate abstaining from foods which God has created to be gratefully shared in by those who believe and know the truth." Paul can't be referring to God's Law as doctrines of demons since it comes directly from God, can he?

In 1 Timothy 4, Paul writes, "paying attention to deceitful spirits and doctrines of demons, men who forbid marriage and advocate abstaining from foods which God has created to be gratefully shared in by those who believe and know the truth." Doesn't Leviticus 11 point out what God defines as food?

1 Timothy 1:8-11 states that the Law of God is good and educates everyone who acts contrary to its sound teaching.

Why do we often hear that obedience to the Law of God is not good and contrary to sound teaching?

We know that Christ says that the greatest commands are "Love God with all your heart and love your neighbor as yourself". Is there any command in the Law of God that doesn't fall under these parameters?

We as believers are obviously encouraged to follow the 10 commandments. Why are we often discouraged to follow the *explanation* of the 10 commandments found in the books following Exodus?

Galatians 5:16-17 says, "But I say, walk by the Spirit, and you will not carry out the desire of the flesh. For the flesh sets its desire against the Spirit, and the Spirit against the flesh; for these are in opposition to one another, so that you may not do the things that you please." Why do we think Galatians is teaching us not to obey God's Law when Romans 7:14 states that it's Spiritual and against the flesh?

Deuteronomy 11:13-17 speaks about obedience to the commands of God in order to acquire rain in its proper season. This is mirrored in the millennial reign of Christ in Zechariah 14:16-21. Why do we often teach that this is something that we're not to do now?

Titus 3:9 says, "...Avoid foolish controversies, genealogies, dissensions, and quarrels about the law, for they are unprofitable and worthless". However, the Savior says in Matthew 5:19: "Whoever then annuls one of the least of these commandments, and teaches others to do the same, shall be called least in the kingdom of heaven; but whoever keeps and teaches them, he shall be called great in the kingdom of heaven." Do these contradict?

Every covenant has terms which we must abide by to keep from breaking the covenant. What are the terms of the new covenant?

Romans 15:4 says, "For whatever was written in earlier times was written for our instruction, so that through perseverance and the encouragement of the Scriptures we might have hope". Doesn't that mean that the Law of God was written for our instruction?

In Hebrews 8:7 and 8:13, we can see that the word Covenant is not there in the Greek but is added by translators. Without the translator bias, doesn't the context suggest a faulty priesthood? Is it more likely that the human priests are faulty, or that God made a faulty covenant?

In John 8:42-47, Christ says that the Devil is a liar and the father of lies, but Christ speaks the truth of God and is without sin. Aren't all of God's commands truth as Psalm 119:151 says? Doesn't Christ only teach what God has instructed, as John 7:16 states?

Isaiah 66:22-24 says that after the New Heaven and New Earth, The Sabbath will still be kept. Matthew 5:17-19 says that the Law of God mentions that we're to keep the Law of God until the New Heaven and New Earth. Why do many Churches disregard the Sabbath and the Law of God?

People often say that Christ redeemed us from obedience to God's Law. How does that make sense when before we had faith in Christ, we were walking in rebellion to God's Law?

If Psalm 51:6 links truth and wisdom together and Psalm 119:43 says God's law is truth and Psalm 119:98 says the Law of God makes one wise, then wouldn't disregarding the Law of God be untrue and unwise?

Why do we often say that the Law of God was too hard for us to follow, but in Deuteronomy 30:11-14, God says, ""For this commandment which I command you today is not too difficult for you, nor is it out of reach"?

Deuteronomy 30:6 says, "Moreover the Lord your God will circumcise your heart and the heart of your descendants, to love the Lord your God with all your heart and with all your soul, so that you may live." How is this different than the definition of the New Covenant?

We're often told that in the New Covenant, we have circumcised hearts instead of the flesh and in the Old Covenant, the people were circumcised in the flesh. Doesn't

Deuteronomy 10:16 speak to a circumcised heart and in Acts 16:3 Paul circumcised Timothy in the flesh?

In 1 Timothy 18-11, we see that the Law of God is only for those who sin and 1 John 1:8 says "If we say that we have no sin, we are deceiving ourselves and the truth is not in us." Wouldn't that indicate that the Law of God is for us to teach us how to live as Christ since sin is breaking God's Law?

In Jeremiah 14:14, God says, "The prophets are prophesying falsehood in My name. I have neither sent them nor commanded them nor spoken to them; they are prophesying to you a false vision, divination, futility and the deception of their own minds." And Deuteronomy 13:4-5 says that we know they're false because they're not teaching obedience to the Law/commands of God. Are we certain we're not teaching falsely in church?

God says in Jeremiah 6:16, "Stand by the ways and see and ask for the ancient paths, Where the good way is, and walk in it; And you will find rest for your souls. But they said, 'We will not walk in it'." Aren't those ways His Laws, and the ancient paths His commandments? Are we still saying we will not walk in it?

In Exodus 18, we see Moses teaching the commands of God before he went up Sinai; are we to believe that the commands are different then what He received on Sinai?

Is the Spirit of God mentioned in Ezekiel 36:26-27 different from the one given to us today, and if so, why is this passage quoted in Hebrews? If not, then isn't the Law of God on our hearts if we're New Covenant believers?

Matthew 24:20-21 points to the Sabbath being kept at a specific time, and Luke 23:52-56 shows that people still kept the Sabbath according to the commandment. Where does the idea that the Sabbath is not to be kept, or that we get to pick "a" Sabbath come from?

In Matthew 15:1-14, Jesus labels the Pharisees as "blind guides" and "hypocrites" for teaching their own doctrines instead of God's commands. Are we sure we're not doing the same things?

Zechariah 14:16-21 mentions that in that time, there will be inscribed on the bells of the horses, "Holy to the Lord." Do we believe that this has happened yet or not?

Is Isaiah 56:6-8 about Jews or Gentiles, and has it happened yet? If not, then shouldn't we do what it says?

Isaiah 51:7 is an encouragement for those who keep the Law of God to not be dismayed by those who mock. Are we as a church more like the ones being encouraged or the ones mocking?

1 Corinthians 15 mentions that Christ is the first fruit and Leviticus 26:10-14 mentions that First Fruits is to be a statute throughout our generations. Why do we not teach about First Fruits in church?

If we were to interpret Mark 7 as Christ making all animals clean, and Revelation 18:2 says that there are still unclean animals, don't those contradict? And if so, shouldn't we rethink how we are interpreting Mark 7?

1 Peter 1:25 says that the Word of the Lord stands forever. Why then do we interpret His commands as being rendered not to be observed?

In Revelation 3:15-16, we see the Savior says that He's going to judge our deeds as hot or cold. What deeds is He speaking of if not obedience to the commands of God?

Colossians 2:9 states, "For in Him all the fullness of Deity dwells in bodily form". Is it possible for Christ to be God and disregard God's Law without God changing or going against His own word?

Colossians 2:8 is often quoted to suggest that the Law of God is not to be observed, but is the Law of God based on the traditions of men/the world or is it from God?

If Ananias and Sapphira were under grace of the New Covenant the way its commonly taught in churches, why were they struck down?

If in Jeremiah 10:3-5 God outlines that cutting a tree down and decorating it is a pagan practice that we're not to do, and Job 14:4 says that no one can make a clean thing out of an unclean thing, why do Christians do this every December?

Ephesians 6:14 says to gird your loins with truth, and Psalm 119:151 says that all of God's commands are truth. Doesn't that mean that equipping the commands is part of the full armor of God?

It's commonly taught that before Jesus, people followed the Law to be saved. But Psalm 130 says that David looked forward to Christ for Salvation. If they never looked to the Law of God for Salvation, then what is it for?

In Isaiah 8:20, we see that if you don't speak to the Law and the testimony, it's because you don't have light, and Ephesians 5:8-10 says to walk in the light, wouldn't that equate light with obeying God's commands? Can light be darkness?

Nehemiah 9:13 says that God's Laws are just and good. Why do we interpret them as oppressive and bad?

In Deuteronomy 18:18, we see that Jesus was to teach the same Word of God as Moses. In John 5:46-47, we see Jesus says the same thing. Why do we say that Jesus taught something different than Moses/the commands of God?

If the Feast of Tabernacles or Sukkot was only for the Jews, as some say, why does Deuteronomy 16:13-15 say that it is also for the gentiles?

In Deuteronomy 10:12-13, God asks us to love Him and walk in all of His ways out of that love. Why do we say that God asks us to ignore parts of that walk?
In Deuteronomy 8:3, we see that man lives not on bread alone but every word that comes out of the mouth of God. Christ quotes this to rebuke the Devil. Why do we say that some of those words of God are not for us?

Why does God want people to follow his commandments always and forever as Deuteronomy 5:29-33 states, if God didn't actually mean always and forever?

In Numbers 15:15, we see that the Law of God is to be a perpetual statute throughout the generations of both Jews and Gentiles alike. Does perpetual mean everlasting or limited?

If everyone was spit out of the land into the Diaspora because they rejected God's Law, then how is the Diaspora to repent from rejecting God's Law if God did away with it?

If Scripture states that the Sabbath is a fixed appointed time of God on the 7th day, why do pastors say that it changed? Who changed it?

How did Cain and Abel know what and when to sacrifice, and God reject Cain's?

In Acts 11, why did Peter keep telling everyone the vision was about gentiles, if it was about eating unclean animals? Why wouldn't he mention eating unclean animals as the interpretation anywhere?

If there is supposed to be a rapture of the saints, why do believers and unbelievers continue to live on the earth like Zechariah 14 teaches?

Wouldn't adding Christmas and Easter as Biblical holidays, while not teaching the Biblical ones, be adding to and taking away from the Word of God?

If Romans 15:4 says whatever was written in former days was written for our instruction, does that mean that rejecting the Law of God is rejecting God's instructions is denying the Scriptures?

2 Timothy 4:3-4 says the time is coming when people will not endure sound teaching and Proverbs 4:2 says good doctrine is keeping to God's Law. Does that mean those who teach against God's Law are teaching a false doctrine?

Why does Jesus tell us to follow the Torah (Moses) without hypocrisy in Matthew 23:2-3 if following the Torah is not for the followers of Jesus?

Why would the alien/gentile be cut off from Israel in Numbers 15:30-31 if the alien/gentile was not part of Israel?

If the Law of God was bondage, why would God lead them out of Egyptian slavery just to give them bondage?

If James 2:10 says that if we break one law, we are guilty of breaking the whole Law. Where do pastors get the idea that there are three different classifications (moral/civil/ceremonial) of the Law.

If Revelation 22:14 says following His commands are a blessing, why do we teach that it's a burden?

Why does Paul, the apostle to the gentiles, tell them to keep the Passover in 1 Corinthians 5:7-8, and why don't we do that now?

Why are there sacrifices when Jesus comes back as in Zechariah 14:16-21?

If the Law is not to be followed, why are we supposed to keep it until Judgment Day, as Malachi 4:4-5 states?

If 2 Corinthians 6:14-18 says to not be unclean, where do we get the definition of clean and unclean, and has that changed from the Torah?

Why is Moses (Law of God) taught every Sabbath (Acts 15:21) in the synagogues to gentiles if gentiles weren't to study the Law of God or keep the Sabbath on the 7th day?

Why do we interpret Paul as saying something different than what God says, and shouldn't we be more attentive to God than Paul in regards to God's Law?

If Proverbs 28:9 says that ignoring God's law/instructions/commands make even your prayer an abomination, when did God change His mind about that?

In Proverbs 3:34 we see that there is grace in the Old Testament. Why do we often hear that grace is a New Testament idea, wouldn't that suggest God changed?

God says in Isaiah 31:2 that He doesn't retract his word, Why would we think the Law of God is not to be followed?

If Daniel 7:25 says that the adversary seeks to change the Law and appointed times of God, are we teaching that Jesus is against God?

If Hebrews 10:1 says that the Law is a good thing to come in heaven, why do we interpret it as bondage? Does that mean that heaven is bondage?

If in Titus 2:11-14 we see that grace redeems us from every lawless deed, why do we present grace as the opposite of the Law instead of its companion?

If Paul says in Romans 6 that we are not to live in sin because we are in Christ, and sin is transgression of the Law, wouldn't that mean that we are to live in obedience to the Law because we are in Christ?

If we are to be redeemed from sin, and sin is transgression of the Law as stated in 1 John 3:4, then wouldn't that mean that our goal is to begin obeying the Law?

If in Acts 10 we are to interpret Peter's vision as Christ making all animals clean, why does Revelation 18:2 say that there are still unclean animals?

If the commands of God are not to be followed, why does Revelation 14:12 say that we are to keep both the commands of God *and* have faith in Jesus?

If Jesus followed the Law of God, and we are called to follow Jesus' example, how do we do that without following the Law of God that was His example?

Why did the false witnesses say Jesus and Stephen were teaching against God's Law in Acts 6:10-15, but we teach that Jesus was teaching us not to follow God's Law?

Why was Paul performing a sacrifice after the death and resurrection of Christ in Acts 21:17-26 to prove that there is no truth to the rumor that he was teaching people not to follow God's Law, if he was teaching people not to follow God's Law?

If Peter tells us to not interpret Paul's writings as teaching us *not* to obey God's Law in 2 Peter 3:14-17, why do we interpret Paul's writings as teaching us not to obey God's Law?

If Jesus in Mark 7 is telling people to ignore God saying what is and isn't food, isn't He teaching us to *not* obey God? Why would Jesus be rebuking the Pharisees in Mark 7 for *not* obeying God's commands, if He was teaching us in that passage to ignore God's commands?

If Acts 10, Peter's vision about the unclean animals, is to be interpreted as God changing His mind about calling pigs unclean, why is He still mad about it in Isaiah 66, and what is to stop Him from changing his mind about any of the promises He's made? Why wouldn't He change His Mind about Salvation or coming back?

If 2 Thessalonians 2 says the *anti*-Christ is the lawless one who deceives others to be lawless (teaching not to obey God's Law), why are those actions being ascribed to Jesus?

If Israel is only the Jews, why does Revelation 7 talk about all of the tribes, not just Judah? If gentiles aren't part of Israel, why does Jesus only say He came for the lost sheep of the house of Israel in Matthew 15:24? Was He bearing false witness, or are gentiles part of Israel?

EXTRA BONUS CHAPTER

The Apologeticist

This is something that I put together when I was really looking to understand why I believe what I believe. The short version of what I believe is that God doesn't change, scripture doesn't conflict, and that Jesus only says and does what the Father says and does. Also, that all scripture is relevant for the life of the believer, teaching what is holy and what isn't. So that being said, read at your own discretion.

Here are the three basic rules that I follow, along with most believers, which will be essential in showing how my search for truth was conducted.

Rule number 1)

God does not change. He does not change his mind. He does not go against his own word.

Rule number 2)

Jesus only said and did the things that God has told him to say and do.

Rule number 3)

Scriptures do not contradict.

95% of Believers would agree to these three points.

From these three points I ask one question with several sub questions that lead to the original inquiry. It is from these three points that I sought to compare denominational doctrine against scripture.

Is the Bible inconsistent? If yes, then it is fallible and merely another book and not inspired by God. If not (which I believe), then one must rectify specific questions.

Why don't we as Christians keep the Dietary instructions as God prescribed them?

A) If God said that it was okay to eat such things as pork and shellfish and owl, then this is a violation of Rules 1 & 3, as God has said that pork and shellfish and owl are not food for man (Leviticus 11).

B) Peter had a vision (Acts 10) where a sheet was lowered with all kinds of animals and God said to him, "rise, kill and eat." If we were to say God was telling Peter that it was now alright to eat unclean animals, then this would be a violation of rules 1 & 3.

Furthermore, the passage states that Peter was confused about the vision (Acts 10:28). Peter starts to get a clue that this had nothing to do with food and everything to do with gentile inclusion in the kingdom (Acts 10:28). In verse 34, it seems to come together for him. We see that Peter is now giving a detailed account of his vision to show that it was not about food, but about not showing partiality (Acts 11).

C) If we are to say that in Mark 7, Christ made all foods clean, including unclean animals, this would violate rules 1, 2, and 3. It would mean that either Jesus was teaching something that God said was not to be done, or that God changed his mind about unclean animals being food for us...which then results in the conflict of scripture. As per Mark 7 passage, verse 3 states that the subject in question was a tradition making something that God had already said was food unclean. This is restated in verse 5. In verses 8, 9, and 13, Jesus rebukes them for setting aside the commands of God, which would be folly if he himself were teaching something against the commands of God— i.e. dietary laws.

D) If we are to say that through Christ's death and resurrection all things can now be eaten because they are now clean, this would violate all three rules as the actions of Jesus would now conflict with the words of God. Also, there is a passage that talks about an outpouring of wrath on those who eat things which God has stated are an abomination. This event has yet to happen therefore one must deduce that this is an event to come (Isaiah 66:16-18). Christ would not execute such wrath if he had deemed these things acceptable.

Why don't people keep the Sabbath the way that God said to keep it?

(A) If we are to say that it has now changed to Sunday, this violates 1 and 3, as the scripture states that the Sabbath is the 7th day, and not the first. Furthermore, Paul tells people to collect money and conduct business on the first day, which would mean that if in fact the Sabbath was changed to the first day, Paul is telling people to violate it by conducting business. There is also no scripture that suggests that the Sabbath was transferred to the first day. Also, the Catholic church makes it very clear that there is no scriptural support for the change of the Sabbath from the 7th day to the 1st, and they take full responsibility for that change.

(B) If we are to say that the Sabbath was part of the Law and the Law is not to be followed anymore, this violates all 3 rules as God states that the commands are to be a perpetual ordinance for Jew and gentile alike, throughout their generations (Exodus 12:49, Exodus-31:16, Galatians 3:29, Ephesians-2:19). Jesus kept the Sabbath, and if we are to follow his perfect example, we would keep the Sabbath as well. To say that it is a perpetual sign for believers, but has been revoked, is inconsistent. Plus, there is support from the books of Hebrews that the Sabbath is still in place (Hebrews-4:9-11). In further support, Isaiah 56 shows that the Sabbath is still in place after the Messiah brings salvation. It is also stated that the Sabbath is in place in heaven (Isaiah 66:22-23) as it endures from the new heaven and new earth, which have not yet been made as pointed out in other passages (2 Peter- 3:10,2 Peter 3:14 Revelation 21:1).

(C) If we are to say that we do keep the Sabbath on Sunday, then this doesn't exactly violate any of the 3 rules, but is a blatant ignoring of the scriptures on the subject of Sabbath keeping. The Sabbath is a day where man is to cease form his efforts and his control. This cannot be done while still choosing what day one wants the Sabbath to be. Also, God states that it is his Sabbath, therefore we do not have control over it. (Isaiah-58:13). The Sabbath is also defined as an appointed time of God, in which the anti-christ seeks to change the times of (Daniel 7:25-26).

(D) If we are to say that Jesus broke the Sabbath, then this is a violation of rules 2 and 3. Jesus kept the Sabbath, as was his custom (Luke-4:16), and if He broke the Sabbath, then He did not do as He has seen the Father do (John 5:19, John 7:16, John 8:28, John 12:49) and would not be the sinless Messiah, but rather be acting like the anti-messiah.

Why don't people follow the law of God?

(A) If we are to say that we are now under Grace, this would imply that there was a time that we were not under grace, and thus would be a violation of rule number 1. There are several points in the Old Testament where grace is prevalent, as grace is loving kindness or unmerited favor (Psalms 103:4, Psalms 103:11, Psalms 103:17, Psalms 130:4, Psalms 130:7).

(B) If we are to say the law was for salvation, then this violates rules 2 and 3, as scripture states that by the law no man was saved, and in Hebrews it states that the sacrifices could never take away sins (Hebrews 11). Plus, King David stated that he looked to the Messiah for salvation as he followed God's law (Psalms-119:166, Psalm 119:81). Also, there was an issue in Acts where a new idea was introduced that some people were saying that one had to be circumcised and ordered to keep all the commandments in Acts 15. This is refuted in the same passage, as it is pointed out that the law was never for salvation (Acts 15:10) but obedience is the result of salvation.

(C) If we are to say that the Law has been done away with or fulfilled (by interpretation of fulfilled meaning rendered into a manner of non-observance), then this is a violation of rules 1 and 3. Jesus stated that he didn't come to abolish the law (Matthew-5:17-19) but to fulfill it. If the word fulfill meant to render into a manner of non-observance, then that would have the same effect as abolishment. He also states that anyone who teaches others not to follow the commands will be least in the kingdom (Matthew-5:19). Plus, how could Jesus have rebuked the Pharisees for setting aside the commands of God, if he was going to set aside the commands of God, and therefore break the three rules?

(D) If we are to say that the Law is bondage, this is a violation of rule 3 since it is stated that the law is liberty (James 1:25, James 2:12, Psalms 119:44-45) and that the law is perfect (James 1:25, Psalm 19:7). Also, if Jesus lived this perfectly and we are called to follow in his footsteps (1 John- 2:6, John-14:21, John-14:15, John 14:12) how would living a life like Christ be bondage?

(E) If we are to say that the Law is too difficult to follow, then this is a violation of all three rules because God stated that it wasn't, as scripture points out (Deuteronomy 30:1, Deuteronomy-30:14). This would also mean that walking the way Jesus walked is too difficult, which is not what the Messiah says (Matthew 11:30).

(F) If we are to say that Paul and the disciples taught against following the Law, then this is a violation of rule 3. Paul only taught against following the law for salvation, not as a result of salvation. Paul himself followed God's law, delighting in it and teaching it, going so far as to perform a vow and sacrifice to show that there is no truth to this teaching (Acts-24:14-15, Acts 21:17-26, Acts-24:18, Acts 26:4-5, Acts-28:23, Romans-7:22, Romans 7:25, 1 Corinthians 9:21, 1 Corinthians 14:37). It was known that the enemies of the disciples were the ones saying that they were teaching against the law of God (Acts 6:10-15). If you note that in verse 14 of Acts 6, these liars state that Jesus was altering the Law, but according to Jesus' words, he doesn't (John-5:46-47).

(G) If we are to say that we now live by the spirit instead of the Law, this would somewhat be in conflict with rule 1, for the spirit of God would never tell you to do something contrary to the Word of God. Plus, the law is spiritual (Romans 7:14).

(H) We are called to be without sin, but this is impossible without following the Law as sin is defined as the violation of God's Law (1 John-3:4). God's grace is defined as redeeming us from every lawless deed (Titus-2:11-14).

How does a dispensation approach to scripture work?

(A) The Idea of having seven dispensations would imply that God changes, which would violate rule 1.

(B) We then have to account for Noah knowing the difference between clean and unclean animals before the dispensations of the Law, where God states what animals are clean and what ones are not clean (Genesis-7:2, Deuteronomy 14, Leviticus 11).

(C) Then we would need to account for the fact that grace is prevalent before the dispensations of grace (Psalms 103:4, Psalms 103:11, Psalms 103:17, Psalms 130:4, Psalms 130:7, Proverbs 3:34).

(D) Additionally, how do we account for the law being returned in the millennial reign of Christ if it is a burden now (Hebrews-10:16, Colossians 2:17, Hebrews- 10:1, Jeremiah 32:40, Isaiah-2:2-3, Zechariah-14:16-21)?

(E) It is also stated that the Holy Spirit was very evident in the lives of believers before the dispensation of grace (Mark 12:36, Exodus 31:3, Numbers 11:16-17).

Do the writings of Paul tell us a different story?

(A) If Romans 14 states that we can eat whatever animals we want, this would violate rules 1 & 3. If we were to look at the terminology as per what defines one who is weak in the faith and cross reference that with other passages of Paul's, we could see that the issue is not about eating unclean animals, but about eating meat that was sacrificed (1 Corinthians 8:9-13). In verse 15 of Romans 14, Paul points out that we are not to cause offense over food, if he was saying unclean animals were food then he would be violating rule 3.

(B) If one were to say that the book of Galatians is telling us not to follow the Law of God, then this would violate rules 1, 2, and 3, as God states that the Law was to be followed by Jew and Gentile alike forever (Numbers 15:15-16, Numbers 15:29). Jesus states that we are to follow everything that the teachers of the Law teach (but not to be hypocrites) (Matthew-23:2-3). If God said to follow the Law, then who is Paul to say something different? We can see in Galatians 2:4 that Paul is writing this letter to refute the teaching that arose in Acts 15; this is restated in Galatians 5:4, since the issue in acts was men seeking to be justified by the Law. In Acts 15, the act of seeking to be justified by the Law was a new heretical doctrine that was introduced, as Peter pointed out that it was a burden that no one in history was asked to bear (Acts 15:9-11).

(C) If one were to say that by getting circumcised it invalidates Christ, this would violate rules 1 and 3. Why did Paul have Timothy circumcised if such an action would be dooming him (Acts 16:3)? But as it were, the issue at hand was relying on the Law when one should have been relying on Christ as they follow the Law. Paul also states that circumcision and uncircumcision are nothing, but what matters is keeping the commands of God (1 Corinthians 7:19), which includes circumcision.

(D) If someone were to imply that we are now circumcised by the heart as an implication that something changed, this would break rule 3, if it were not already something that was in place (Deuteronomy 10:16, Leviticus 26:41, Jeremiah 4:4).

(E) If Paul were teaching that we should not follow the Law of God, then he would have been guilty of taking away from the commands of God (Deuteronomy -4:2, Deuteronomy 5:29-33, Deuteronomy-12:32), and therefore breaking rule 3. We see that Paul states that he agrees with everything written in the Law and he follows it (Acts-24:14-15, Acts 26:4-5).

(F) If someone were to suggest that Paul teaches that we do not hold believers accountable in regards to what they eat or regarding the Sabbath, this would be in violation of rule 3. We find a notion of this in Colossians 2:16. However, if this is an admonishment of keeping the Sabbath or any of God's Law, then Paul could not refer to it as hollow and deceptive philosophy (Colossians 2:8). This would also conflict with his own words, as he writes to Timothy that all scripture is for rebuke, encouragement, and reproof, which breaks rule 3 (2 Timothy-3:14-17). This would include the dietary restrictions, as at the time of him penning those words, the only scriptures that existed were the "Old Testament" in its entirety. Furthermore, it is God's Law and not that of any man and it has always been God's Sabbath.

(G) We also have it under Peter's testimony that Paul does not teach against God's Law (2 Peter- 3:14-17).

(H) How can we adhere to Paul when he says follow me as I follow Christ, if we are to interpret his teachings to say that after we are saved, we shouldn't follow the Law of God, as Christ who we are saved by, followed the Law of God? It is also said in Daniel 7:24-26 that the anti-christ seeks to change the Law and appointed times of God.

What about Revelation?

(A) If the commandments of God are burdensome, and it is one of the roles of the adversary to create burden and strife, why does he hate those who keep the commands of God (Revelation 12:17)? If the commands of God were said to be a burden, then this would violate rules 1 and 3, as God and 1 John say that they are not (1 John 5:3, Deuteronomy-30:11).

(B) If the commands are not to be followed, then why is the perseverance of the saints (us) outlined as those who hold to the commands of God in conjunction with faith in Christ (Revelation-14:12)?

(C) If Christ made all animals clean, then why does Revelation 18:2 still list unclean birds? Why does Revelation 21:27 state that those who commit abominations and nothing unclean can draw near, if eating unclean things had somehow been all made clean? If God had changed his mind about eating unclean things being an abomination, why is this same thing paralleled in Isaiah 66 as an end times event?

REFERENCED WORKS

A.R. Fausset Bible dictionary Passover- citing Josephus (B. J., 6:9, section 3)

Davidson, Richard M. "Condemnation and Grace: Polygamy and Concubinage in the Old Testament" (2015). Faculty Publications. (69)

Ensley, Joshua
https://x.com/JoshuaEnsleyOrg/status/1693046424500326711

Codex Justinianeus.
https://ancientinsights.wordpress.com/2022/08/29/scripture-forbids-polygamy/

Eusebius. Church History, Book V, Chapter 24. Translated by Arthur Cushman McGiffert. Excerpted from Nicene and Post-Nicene Fathers, Series Two, Volume 1. Edited by Philip Schaff and Henry Wace. American Edition, 1890. Online Edition Copyright © 2004 by K. Knight.

https://www.biblegateway.com/quicksearch/?quicksearch=christmas&version=NASB1995

https://www.blueletterbible.org/lexicon/g113/nasb20/mgnt/0-1/

https://www.blueletterbible.org/lexicon/g4074/nasb20/mgnt/0-1/

https://www.blueletterbible.org/lexicon/g5293/nasb20/mgnt/0-1/

https://www.blueletterbible.org/lexicon/h3627/nasb20/wlc/0-1/

https://www.blueletterbible.org/lexicon/h4910/nasb20/wlc/0-1/

https://www.blueletterbible.org/lexicon/h4910/nasb20/wlc/0-1/

https://www.blueletterbible.org/lexicon/h5048/nasb20/wlc/0-1/

https://www.blueletterbible.org/lexicon/h5248/nasb20/wlc/0-1/
https://www.blueletterbible.org/lexicon/h2154/nasb20/wlc/0-1/

https://www.blueletterbible.org/lexicon/h5303/nasb20/wlc/0-1/

https://www.blueletterbible.org/lexicon/h5307/kjv/wlc/0-1/

https://www.blueletterbible.org/lexicon/h7218/nasb20/wlc/0-1/

https://www.blueletterbible.org/nasb20/gen/2/1/t_conc_2018

https://www.rogersteer.com/boniface-and-the-story-of-the-christmas-tree/

https://www.spurgeon.org/resource-library/sermons/the-first-christmas-carol/#flipbook/

https://www.spurgeongems.org/sermon/chs1026.pdf

Josephus, Flavius. The Wars of the Jews William Whiston, A.M., Ed.

Joy Born at Bethlehem, Charles Haddon Spurgeon December 23, 1871 Scripture: Luke 2:10, 11, 12 From: Metropolitan Tabernacle Pulpit Volume 17

Justin Martyr Dialogue with Trypho (Chapters 31-47) Translated by Marcus Dods and George Reith. From Ante-Nicene Fathers, Vol. 1.

Edited by Alexander Roberts, James Donaldson, and A. Cleveland Coxe. (Buffalo, NY: Christian Literature Publishing Co., 1885.) Revised and edited for New Advent by Kevin Knight.

Philo, Special Laws I, XXXV (169) Philo of Alexandria (a.k.a. Philo Judaeus, ca. 15 BCE–50 CE

Supplementa Calviniana, volume 5, sermons on Micah, p. 172, lines 20ff, translated from French by The Ranter. Preaching, Praying and Policing the Reform in Sixteenth-Century Geneva, unpublished Ph.D. dissertation by Thomas A. Lambert, University of Wisconsin-Madison, 1998

The Catholic Encyclopedia (P.L., XXXVIII, 1024 sqq.; Serm. cxcvii, cxcviii) Acta SS., Jan., I, Sermo Faustini (describing secular festivities and Christian fasts; BUTLER, The Lives of the Saints, 1 Jan.; SMITH, Dict. of Christ. Antiquities, s.v.; DUCHESNE, Les origines du culte chrét. (tr. London, 1904), 273.

The First Christmas Carol, Charles Haddon Spurgeon December 20, 1857

Works of Lucian Vol. IV: Saturnalia p.108 https://sacred-texts.com/cla/luc/wl4/wl422.htm

ABOUT THE AUTHOR

J.M. Muratore was born in Phoenix, Arizona, but spent his youth and young adult years living in various cities. At the age of ten, he embraced the promise that God would never leave or forsake him, accepting Christ and beginning a lifelong journey of faith. At nineteen, he developed a deep passion for studying God's grace and Biblical Law within the framework of His unchanging nature—a pursuit that has continued for over two decades.

When he's not writing or engaging in online apologetics, Muratore enjoys exploring local restaurants and coming up with creative nicknames for his sister's dog, Bailey—favorites include "Fartato" and "Burrito Face." He currently resides in northern Idaho, where he shares his insights and studies on God through his blog, The Giant Slayer.

To learn more visit:
https://therealgiantslayer.blogspot.com/2012/09/oh-you-know-just-some-study-notes.html?m=1

www.ingramcontent.com/pod-product-compliance
Lightning Source LLC
Chambersburg PA
CBHW031827090426
42741CB00005B/159